Praise for Margo Jefferson's

ON MICHAEL JACKSON

"Jefferson is onto something. . . . By the time I finished this slim volume, I found that [she] had won me over with her erudite compassion for this fragile circus figure."　—Kyle Smith, *The Wall Street Journal*

"Trenchant. . . . Thought-provoking. . . . Interesting insights."　　　　　　　　　　—*USA Today*

"Sparkling. . . . Eloquent and provocative. . . . Proves how much a smart and thoughtful writer can find to say on a subject that—we wrongly might have assumed—we've already heard too much about. . . . Watching Margo Jefferson's mind at work is as pleasurable and thrilling as seeing Michael Jackson dance."

—*O, The Oprah Magazine*

"[Jefferson] resists the quicker shortcuts of pop-culture punditry. . . . A book [close] in spirit to a performance by the King of Pop himself—something graceful, capable of moves both liquid and percussive, dancing across the rooftops of cultural history."

—*Newsday*

"Provocative and insightful."　　　—*The Seattle Times*

"Wise, nuanced.... Journalism crossed with poetry....
Jefferson writes the way Jackson, in his prime, used to
dance—with elegance and attitude."

—*The Washington Post*

"Insightful.... Regardless of how one feels about Jackson these days—misunderstood genius or sideshow
attraction—Jefferson's book is a pop culture must-
read."   —*The Sacramento Bee*

"[An] effective treatise.... Jefferson, in quick, cut-to-
the-bone strokes, examines Michael's bizarre, brutal
working childhood and adolescence, and how that
formed and deformed his own and the public's image
of him.... This book is a serious book."

—*New York Post*

"What Jefferson lyrically and skillfully does here is
give us fleeting, disconnected scenes from Jackson's
life and background.... Her precise, evocative prose
is a pleasure to read."   —*The Baltimore Sun*

"Expertly crafted—and by turns extremely hilari-
ous.... A remarkable treatise."

—*Black Issues Book Review*

"Few have been able to piece together the complex puzzle of Jackson's life, let alone place it into a social context. . . . *On Michael Jackson* is a powerful analysis of Jackson the icon and goes beyond the tabloid journalism to look at the man and his life."   *—Ebony*

"Thoughtful. . . . Sharp. . . . [*On Michael Jackson*] has the kind of authority . . . to last well into an era when people might not know his looks, but may well still be enjoying his music."   *—Houston Chronicle*

"Margo Jefferson . . . has given Michael Jackson's career, persona and self-destruction the meditative weight and lament they deserve. It's an uncommonly graceful little book."   *—The Buffalo News*

"Displays a lively understanding of black performing history. . . . [Jefferson] is enough of a writer to convince one, rather quickly, that the big-hearted, firm-minded essay . . . may be the place where [issues of cultural studies] can begin to find their most open-ended resolution."   *—London Review of Books*

"Few have been able to piece together the complex puzzle of Jackson's life, let alone place it in a social context.... On Michael Jackson is a powerful analysis of Jackson the icon and goes beyond the rabid fan fanaticism to look at the man and his life." —Ebony

"Thoughtful ... sharp.... [On Michael Jackson] has the kind of authority ... to last well into an era when people might not know his looks, but may well still be enjoying his music." —Houston Chronicle

"Margo Jefferson ... has given Michael Jackson's career persona and self-destruction the meditative weight and lament they deserve. It's an uncommonly graceful little book." —The Buffalo News

"Displays a lively understanding of black performing history.... [Jefferson] is enough of a writer to convince one, rather quickly, that the big-hearted, broad-minded essay ... may be the place where [issues of cultural studies] can begin to find their most open-ended resolution." —London Review of Books

Margo Jefferson

On Michael Jackson

Margo Jefferson was a staff critic for *The New York Times* from 1993 to 2006. She received the Pulitzer Prize in 1995. Her reviews and essays have also appeared in *The Nation*; *Grand Street*; *O, The Oprah Magazine*; *The Village Voice*; *Vogue*; *American Theatre*; *Dance Ink*; and *Harper's Magazine*. She teaches at Columbia University and Eugene Lang College at The New School University, and lives in New York City.

ON
MICHAEL
JACKSON

ON
MICHAEL
JACKSON

Margo Jefferson

Vintage Books
A Division of Random House, Inc.
New York

FIRST VINTAGE BOOKS EDITION, JANUARY 2007

Copyright © 2006 by Margo Jefferson

All rights reserved. Published in the United States by Vintage Books,
a division of Random House, Inc., New York, and in Canada
by Random House of Canada Limited, Toronto. Originally
published in hardcover in the United States by Pantheon Books,
a division of Random House, Inc., New York, in 2006.

Vintage and colophon are registered trademarks of
Random House, Inc.

The Library of Congress has cataloged the
Pantheon edition as follows:
Jefferson, Margo, [date]
On Michael Jackson / Margo Jefferson.
p.   cm.
1. Jackson, Michael, 1958—Criticism and interpretation.
2. Jackson, Michael, 1958—Psychology. 3. Popular music—
Social aspects—United States. 4. Popular culture. I. Title.
ML420.J175J44 2006
782.42166'092—dc22
2005053489

Vintage ISBN: 978-0-307-27765-7

Author Photograph © Brent Murray
Book design by Virginia Tan

www.vintagebooks.com

Printed in the United States of America
10   9   8   7   6   5   4

For Irma Armstrong Jefferson
and in memory of
Ronald Nelson Jefferson

and in memory of

Contents

Contents

ON
MICHAEL
JACKSON

Freaks

Every mind is a clutter of memories, images, inventions and age-old repetitions. It can be a ghetto, too, if a ghetto is a sealed-off, confined place. Or a sanctuary, where one is free to dream and think whatever one wants. For most of us it's both—and a lot more complicated. A ghetto can be a place of vitality; a sanctuary can become a prison. Michael Jackson escaped the ghetto of Gary, Indiana, and built the sanctuary of Neverland. It's become a circuslike prison, emblematic of his mind.

Think of Michael Jackson's mind as a funhouse,[1] and look at some of the exhibits on display: P. T. Barnum, maestro of wonders and humbuggery; Walt Disney, who invented the world's mightiest fantasy-technology complex; Peter Pan ("He escaped from being human when he was seven days old"[2]); a haggard

Edgar Allan Poe (he was the only character besides Peter Pan that Michael Jackson planned to play in a movie); the romping, ever-combustible Three Stooges; a friendly chimpanzee named Bubbles who has his own wardrobe of clothes; and a python lying coiled between placid white llamas.

Tears roll down the gnarled lizard cheeks of E.T. as he dreams of home; Charlie Chaplin sits alone on a stoop, his Little Tramp chin in his hands. A knife gleams in a darkened alley; a panther stalks through and disappears; ghouls and werewolves dance in a crumbling mansion; Captain Eo wears silver when he comes down from outer space to save children from the evils of our planet. Now lines of song-and-dance men kick, strut and turn in perfect unison. Children of all nations float happily through the night sky like Wynken, Blynken and Nod, then come down to earth and sing of peace in high, sweet voices; a colossal statue of Michael Jackson himself in military dress bestrides the world to the rapturous attack chords of "Carmina Burana."

Here is Elvis Presley, who is one of himselves; Diana Ross, who is one of himselves; Elizabeth Taylor, who is one of himselves; wee, nut-brown Emmanuel Lewis and pert, milky-white Macaulay Culkin, both parts of himself; Joseph Jackson, the father who believes in whippings but not beatings; Katherine Jackson, the mother who is always supportive and always

4

elusive. See photos from childhood onward and videos of Michael; they are mirrors reflecting each stage of his life.

Let's begin our tour.

Phineas T. Barnum? A model for Michael. The ringmaster of American entertainment. Fantasy, fakery and touches of uplift. No one knew better than Barnum how to thrill audiences, give them raw sensation and a stirring, not especially accurate education. Barnum's first spectacular success came in 1835, when he bought the rights to exhibit an ex-slave named Joice Heth at his Connecticut theater. Servitude had left her a near cripple; the showman saw promise in those gnarled limbs and stooped shoulders. Barnum put her in a clean gown and a fresh white cap, sat her down and introduced eager crowds to the 161-year-old nurse of George Washington. "To use her own language when speaking of the illustrious Father of his Country, 'she raised him,' " his advertisements proclaimed.

When Heth died the next year, Barnum ordered a public autopsy. An unexpectedly honest doctor revealed that, far from being born in 1674, Heth was no more than eighty years old. Barnum professed astonishment. He'd been conned by Heth and her ex-master, he declared. Then his business partner upped the ante and declared that Barnum had found Heth on a plantation and trained her himself to pass for Washington's nurse. The public enjoyed both tales, and Barnum enjoyed spreading both tales. People wanted to believe *and* know they'd be conned, as long as they didn't know when or how.

In 1842, Barnum opened his American Museum on lower Broadway in New York City. It cost twenty-five cents to get in, not an inconsiderable sum in those days: "One ticket guaranteed admission to lectures, theatrical performances, an animal menagerie and a glimpse of human curiosities, living and dead."[3] An exhibit features Madame Clofullia from Europe. Madame was born in Switzerland. In a photograph she stands quietly in her black ruffled gown, resting a hand gently on her husband's shoulder. There is a bunch of white lace at her throat. But it is partially hidden by her long, dark, bushy beard. An angry museum patron takes her to court. She is a man, he protests. The suit is free advertising for Barnum. He takes a group of physicians to court with him; together they offer medical proof that Madame Clofullia is biologically female. She goes on working at the museum.

It isn't always easy to find genuine human wonders like Madame Clofullia. As a man of the theater, Barnum knows how to turn a startling visual effect into an adventure yarn. Put a tattooed man in a loincloth and he becomes Prince Constentenus of Greece. The prince was kidnapped by the Khan of Kashagar: that is why he has 185 tattoo patterns on his body, each one cruelly carved into his flesh with needles.

Michael Jackson read Barnum's autobiography fervently (at least one of the eight versions) and gave copies to all his staff, telling them, "I want my career to be the greatest show on earth." So he became both producer and product. The impresario of himself. Who among us can't recall at least one of the stunts that followed: Michael sleeping in a hyperbaric chamber like a handsome young pharaoh in his tomb or the lovely Snow White in her glass casket? He was obsessed with the Elephant Man; he claimed he saw the movie thirty-five times, never once without weeping all the way through! He made repeated attempts, offered millions of dollars, to buy the bones from The British Museum. He appeared in public wearing a surgical mask: he could have been the doctor in an old horror film, looming over the evil or tragic man about to have his identity and destiny changed forever. Then we see him without the mask, onstage, at an awards ceremony, in court, and realize he has been that man for a long time.

He became a one-man conglomerate with global reach: his own records and videos; the Beatles' catalog; Pepsi commercials; world tours. He was transnational. He reenacted his supremacy in video after video. "If you wanna be my baby / don't matter if you're black or white." If you want to dance with me, don't matter if you're Indian, Russian, African or Native American. You can morph into anything (pudgy Eskimo into buff, white American lad with straight, honey-blond hair; American lad into slim, brown-skinned lass with dark brown frizzy hair); you can be any age, race or gender. Global idealism is at one with global marketing. If you want to buy my records, don't matter who, what or where you are.

Barnum's museum exhibits, ethnological curiosities and circus sideshows also set the pattern for our daytime talk shows. The difference between then and now? Barnum's people were supposed to be freaks of nature, outside the boundaries of The Normal. Ours are marketed as lifestyle freaks. Psychology and sociology have played as big a part as biology; that's the point of those long confessional interviews with the host and those fraught exchanges with the audience. Nighttime shows like *Fear Factor* are recreational sideshows. Eating slug sandwiches and jumping into sealed tanks turn the old carnival tricks (sword swallowing, biting chickens' heads off) into middle-class pranks. Everyday people indulge their whims and get their hit of fame. More and more, they involve playacting and wish fulfillment: this week you make deals Donald Trump respects; you're the "average Joe" the right woman picks over the handsome stud; your "extreme makeover" turns you from a dog to a babe.

More and more of these shows are updates of the old talent contest. Now, though, the backstage tale, the life story, matters as much as the performance. Maybe more. It's about watching the struggle to be the best that you can be, even when you're preposterous; it's about living out your dream. These stories follow—or long to follow—the arc of Michael's early life. You start small, but you have the talent; you work night and day; you make your way to the big city at last, audition for the right talent scouts and producers. You win a contract and your shot at fame. *Star Search. American Idol. So You Think You Can Dance.*

But Michael Jackson became world-famous because he was a world-class talent. His 1983 performance of "Billie Jean" at the televised tribute *Motown: Yesterday, Today, Forever* placed Michael Jackson against the backdrop of his show-business childhood. The other performers were aging; they looked like they were barely surviving liquor and drug crises, feuds, plain old illness and career lapses. Michael looked like a pristine creation, untainted by that past.

Michael was in profile as the bass line of "Billie Jean" rumbled up: legs apart, knees bent in demi-plié, one hand lightly touching his fedora. A hoofer cavalier in high-water pants. Eight counts of pelvic thrusts turned him into a soul-man cavalier. A quick kick and thigh slap on each side, then he faced the audience and—smack on the beat—threw his hat into the wings. Song-and-dance man. Then he mimicked a fifties bad boy, giving his hair a quick comb.

All the elements of the persona we would come to know were on display. The wardrobe that joined severity (black pants, fedora, loafers) with glitter, sparkle and eccentricity (sweater jacket and shirt, white socks, single white glove). Passion that stirred the audience, yet felt private and mysterious. The intense theatricality and how he stretched small gestures into long lines of movement. Every choreographer has signature moves and combinations. Here was the core of Jackson's style: the angled feet and knock-knees of the Funky Chicken (gritty) and the Charleston (more soigné); various runs and struts; the corkscrew kicks forward (as fast as judo kicks); the spin turns; the moonwalk and the sudden crouch when, instead of falling to his knees, he rises on his toes. It's a ballet moment. And a small variation on that move shifts the tension. When he rises with feet and knees together, he looks powerful. With knees together and feet apart, he looks vulnerable, even stricken.

"Billie Jean" is a song about anxiety and guilt, desire and resentment; fathering a child and being a child. In the bridge, when he sang of how Mama warned him, "Be careful what you do / because a lie becomes the truth," he jumped straight into the air three times. The genie in the bottle is a young man who can't control his energies. In the repeat bridge, as he recalled "the smell of sweet perfume / She brought me to her room," he jumped from foot to foot with his knees up, like a boy having a tantrum.

And finally, as he sang, the expressive arms: arms

outstretched, hands pleadingly open (musical theater melodrama); then an emphatic fist or sudden wrist curl; an index finger piercing the air (chitlin' circuit bravado). He brought one hand across his face when he sang "his eyes were like mine," about the mystery child; we saw his round dark eyes through spread-out fingers (Motown mime). He ended stage center, right arm in the air, looking drained but exalted. He created the show; he *was* the show. Idea man, song-and-dance man, money man. But by the mid-1980s he had a lot of us paying more attention to the freak than to the artist. The producer in him knew something had to be done. The outlet he chose was the daytime talk show, media home for our culture's freaks. The place that invites them in to explain and display their lives to regular folk; justify, flaunt, challenge and beguile. In 1993, when the public questions about Michael Jackson's whitening skin had become clamorous, he appeared on *The Oprah Winfrey Show* to explain that he had vitiligo, a disease that drained the pigment from his skin, leaving white blotches. That's why he had to even it out with thick white makeup.

His was a downward spiral after that. By 2003, when he stood on a hotel balcony high above a crowd of cheering fans and held up his new baby for them to see, people thought he had gone mad—or mad enough to be staging a *Fear Factor* publicity stunt. Actually, if you look closely at the picture, he is holding the baby firmly; there's no real danger of his dropping him. Still, why hold a baby over a balcony for cheering throngs, like royalty showing off a new prince to its subjects? By then only true Michael fanatics considered him the King of Pop.

Come this way. Here are real biological freaks, born, but also self-made. Barnum had a long-running hit with his "Siamese" twins, Chang and Eng (the term a remnant of period Orientalism. Of all the conjoined twins billed as "Siamese" in nineteenth-century circuses and carnivals, they were the only ones actually born in Siam). Onstage, Chang and Eng talked about their lives, sang and let themselves be stared at. Their words showed they were people. But they were creatures, too, mutations, signs that evolution is a game of chance and nature is a trickster.[4]

Chang and Eng had immigrated to the States. But an entrepreneur who wanted exotic specimens from faraway lands couldn't often find the genuine article. So the Joice Heth model prevailed. Shameless fakery with, if possible, a strong dose of the topical. When the Civil War began, Barnum had just put an English circus performer in black makeup and a furry tunic, given him a jungle backdrop and asked the public "What Is It?" In 1875, he put an African-American in the part: William Henry Johnson played the "What Is It?" well into the next century.

"Is it a Lower Order of MAN? Or is it a higher order of MONKEY? None can tell! Perhaps it is a combination of both. It is beyond dispute THE MOST MARVELLOUS CREATURE LIVING, it was captured in a savage state in Central Africa, it is probably about 20 years old, 2 feet high, intelligent, docile, active, sportive and PLAYFUL AS A KITTEN. It has a skull, limbs and general anatomy of an ORANG OUTANG and the COUNTENANCE of a HUMAN BEING."

This is the language of the sideshow with touches of natural-history-museum rhetoric. And, in fact, the claims of science began to challenge those of show business. William Henry Johnson was still playing the missing link between man and ape in 1906, when a group of anthropologists arrived in New York with Ota Benga, a central African Batwa who had been brought to the States two years earlier as part of the Pygmy Village at the St. Louis World's Fair. The scientists put Ota Benga in the monkey house at the Bronx Zoo.

Barnum's love of humbug across racial lines inspired a new generation of show-business entrepreneurs. If circus owners couldn't find genuine dark-skinned specimens, they found physically handicapped white Americans to play them. Anthropologists popularized the idea that being nonwhite meant being at the low end of the evolutionary scale. Some turned their universities into showplaces. Others went into show business and took their specimens onto the vaudeville circuit.

By the 1880s, Americans were mastering the globe, in fact and fiction, from wars to world fairs.

Here's what's astonishing about Michael Jackson today: he contains trace elements of all this history. Some he calculated, some went beyond him. Some trapped him as surely as Ota Benga got trapped behind the bars of the Bronx Zoo. From the mideighties on, he turned himself into a "What Is It?" With genius and generosity as an artist; with solitary and fearsome zeal as a man.

Was he man, boy, man-boy or boy-woman? Mannequin or postmodern zombie? Here was a black person who had once looked unmistakably black, and now looked white or at least un-black. He was, at the very least, a new kind of mulatto, one created by science and medicine and cosmetology. Biology defines a mulatto as the sterile offspring of an animal or plant species. Michael Jackson's sperm count, I'm relieved to say, is one of the few things we know nothing about. We are reasonably certain he chose not to produce offspring by traditional means: here again, science joined nature to do his bidding.

Ah, but the art! He got it all back with his wondrous art. Art orders contradictions and unwelcome longings; glorifies what's perverse or infantile, lavish and dream-bright, suave, abject, incurably romantic. It gives shape and rhythm to inchoate fantasies. Finds a common fund of myth, dreams and nightmares; an archive of shared history. A shared body of sound and movement, too: melodies and beats; phrasings that quicken the blood and shock the nervous system.

When people praise Michael Jackson today, recall his gifts and why they loved him, they always mention the 1983 *Thriller* video. That's because it's a short masterpiece, a perfectly thought-through and executed horror tale. It is the tale of the double, the man with two selves and two souls, like Dr. Jekyll and Mr. Hyde, like Poe's William Wilson or Dorian Gray and his portrait. The everyday man and his uncanny double. Which is his true self? "Everything which ought to have remained secret and hidden, but which has come to light." The everyday man broods and agonizes. Why does he feel a connection to this dreadful menacing other? Why is he drawn to an alien, even criminal life? How does he keep this second self concealed? Does he really want to conceal it, especially from the woman whose love he has sought and won?

Thriller begins as Michael, wearing red leather, walks along a deserted street with a fresh-faced, ponytailed girl in a felt skirt, white blouse and saddle shoes. They are 1950s vintage teenagers. (We rarely saw such Negro boys and girls next door in the 1950s.) "You know I like you," he tells her, shyly but winningly. "And I like you," she says eagerly. "Will you be my girl?" he asks. "Oh, yes," she answers. But there's something he wants to say to her. A shadow crosses his face. "You know I'm not like the other guys," he says, to which she responds, "I know. That's why I like you."

And then, right before her eyes, the transformation. The defacement. He turns from a beautiful young man into a hairy, red-eyed werewolf. She shrieks, turns away and starts to run. He chases her, pins her down; we watch her eyes widen as she stares up at him and waits—often the last moment in a horror film—as the camera focuses on the wide-open eyes of the victim. They're our eyes, of course, but we get to keep watching. So does the girl in *Thriller*. She's us. She keeps getting pulled back to safety so that she can keep watching and loving Michael as he doubles and divides. And then, and then . . . And then we're in a movie theater, watching it all on the screen. Michael and his girl are sitting in the audience. She shivers and hides her face on his shoulder; he munches popcorn and grins at the screen. There's a touch of greed in his eyes.

They leave the theater and begin the long walk home. They approach a deserted mansion. And suddenly monsters begin to appear. Limbs crack through the earth; shadowy figures rise and stalk through the trees. Skeletons and demons gather on the mansion grounds. It's Walpurgisnacht in suburbia. It's movie night too. They dance in unison to a heavy drumbeat, rattling their limbs, sliding across the ground, shoulders scooping up and down, forward and back. The voice of Vincent Price—those ornamented syllables, that cavernous vibrato—can be heard intoning—no, rapping: "The hounds of hell await whosoever shall be found without the soul for getting down." The ghouls and demons rising from the dead, we are told, represent "the funk of forty thousand years."

The girl flees into the mansion and slams the door. To no avail. Heavy fists break through the walls; bodies splinter the door. They move closer and closer; she twists herself into an agonized ball and . . . Silence. "Come on," Michael says with a sweet smile. (She looks up tremulously.) "I'll take you home." He helps her to her feet and, arm round her waist, guides her toward safety. Then turns back to us for one last moment. Red is the color of demons. His smile widens and hardens; his eyes flash yellow. The video ends. The credits roll. Good or evil, human or monster, victim or criminal; on-screen Michael will swap selves forever.

Life is another matter. Moving from art to life, Freud talks about fears we cannot dispel or overcome. The best we can do is repress them. But they return in disguise. They look different, unfamiliar, but we know them; they draw us back in. How could Dr. Jekyll live and work if Mr. Hyde weren't there to act on his beastly, murderous impulses? Dorian Gray could not go on if the portrait weren't there in the attic—and if he couldn't forget about it most of the time.

Art makes all of this bearable, even thrilling. But when art crosses back into life and fantasy becomes biography, we're appalled. That's what happened to Michael Jackson in the 1990s. Even as his music and dance were mattering less and less, his looks, his marriages, his masked children, the first round of sexual abuse charges, the out-of-court settlement, all took center stage. With the onset of the new millennium, there were now reissues of old hits and new charges of sexual abuse. We brought those images to his criminal trial of 2005. By now he had achieved full-blown uncanniness; his double, whoever or whatever it was, seemed to have triumphed. As Freud says: "You can also speak of a living person as uncanny, and we do so when we ascribe evil intentions to him. But that is not all. We must feel that his intentions to harm us are going to be carried out with the help of special powers." But who is Michael Jackson's double? Is it the brown-skinned self we can no longer see except in the old photos and videos? Is he a good man or a predator? Child protector or pedophile? A damaged genius or a scheming celebrity trying to hold on to his fame at any cost? A child star afraid of aging, or a psychotic freak/pervert/sociopath? What if the "or" is an "and"? What if he is all of these things?

Over here, please. We call our next funhouse exhibit "Have You Seen My Childhood?" This little fellow is Tom Thumb. Not the one in *Grimm's Fairy Tales* who outwits thieves and cuts his way through a wolf's belly. No, this is Charles Stratton. He began working for Phineas T. Barnum when he was just five years old. He was a two-foot midget. Barnum taught him to sing, dance and act, then named him General Tom Thumb. At his full height of 33", audiences loved to see him play virile military heroes like Napoléon: he'd march about the stage waving a wooden sword ten inches long; after a tour of Europe he even staged a battle with Queen Victoria's poodle.

The child star and the freak were one and the same. General Tom, the midget child imitating heroically grand soldiers (instead of heroically sexy soul men, as Michael did). It had drama and sentiment. It had the wink of the dirty joke (a sword much smaller than Napoléon's, but far longer than the average erect penis!). However, Tom Thumb grew up on the inside, heeded the demands of his brain, muscles and hormones. At the age of twenty-six he married another show-business midget, "Queen" Lavinia Warren. He aspired to be normal. So did she. And their wedding was mobbed. Fans wanted to look at them and try to imagine just how they would go about becoming man and wife.

People see freaks and think: "How do they do it? What kind of sex lives are available to Siamese twins, hermaphrodites, bearded ladies, and midgets? There is a certain morbid speculation about what it would be like to be with such persons, or worse, to be them."⁵ A lot of child stars fail as adult actors because they cannot convince their public or themselves that they can be desirably sexual. Tom Thumb and Queen Lavinia retired once they had married. General Tom moved into adulthood. Michael Jackson married, had children and moved away from adulthood.

Here's another little man. Bigger than Tom Thumb, but still, only five feet one inch tall. And though he lived to the age of seventy-seven, he kept his black hair to the end—never a trace of gray or white. He is James Barrie, who wrote *Peter Pan*. Peter was a boy who wanted never to grow up; Barrie was a grown-up who longed to be a child and spend his life with children, not other grown-ups. Especially boys like him and his brother David. He married, but the women he loved most were friends and protectors. His childhood ended when he was six and his brother David died. He saw that his mother could not be consoled; she had lost the son she loved best. His childhood never ended because he remained six. He tried to revise his life by forever being the boy who was loved by other boys and loved by their mothers.

Neverland is a happy presexual island ("for the Neverland is always more or less an island") ruled by boys.[6] Grief and loss are at its root. Peter Pan ran away from home when he was seven days old ("he escaped by the window") and settled in Kensington Gardens. "If you think he was the only baby who ever wanted to escape, it shows how completely you have forgotten your own young days." The birds taught him to fly, and he settled in with the fairies and had a fine time dancing and playing his pipes night after night. Eventually he became half human and half bird, "a betwixt-and-between." Sometimes, though, he would visit his house and watch his mother weep; the window was always open. He liked that she missed him, and he wanted to keep his options open. But one night when he arrived expecting a welcome, the window was locked. When he looked in, she was asleep with her arm around another child. "When we reach the window, it is Lock-Out Time. The iron bars are up for life." Devastated, he turned his back on her, flew to Neverland, and turned himself into the island's boy-king. From that day on, he helped other children flee their parents to a life of pleasure and adventure. "I'm youth, I'm joy," he crowed to his enemy, the wicked, unloved Captain Hook. Hook and his pirates were the only adults on the island. Peter and his band of Lost Boys killed them all. But they never discussed fathers. Mothers, he told Wendy, were not to be trusted.

When Jane Fonda told Michael that she wanted to produce *Peter Pan* for him, he began to tremble. He identified so with Peter, he told her; he had read everything written about him. Did he know that the book's original title was *The Boy Who Hated His Mother*? As Michael wrote in his autobiography: "I don't trust anybody except Katherine. And sometimes I'm not so sure about her."

We have to move on now. As we go, please study this replica of P. T. Barnum's first mansion. He commissioned it from the same architect who had built King George's royal pavilion in Brighton. Its "Hindoo" style was reflected Chinese, Japanese, Indian and Moorish design (real or imagined). Barnum gave it the mythical name "Iranistan." Once more he had started a tradition: Iranistan, Disneyland, Graceland, Neverland.

Here are old pictures of Michael at Disneyland in the 1970s. He looks so happy standing next to Mickey Mouse. He watched cartoons for hours, he told interviewers; "I loved being a cartoon," he said about the *The Jackson 5ive* series that turned The Jackson Five into animation idols. It seemed so infantile at the time. ("Do you realize this is someone whose inner life is *Tom and Jerry?*" a psychoanalyst friend said wonderingly.)

Who knew that he was after the power of Walt Disney's imagination and brand, his ability to make magic and money from any kind of setting or creature—a park, a mouse, a duck, an elephant, the heroine of a fairy tale that's been told a thousand times? In 1981, Michael's father sold him fifty percent of Hayvenhurst, the family estate. He made it into a private amusement park. When he moved out of his parents' house, he filled his new place with toys and animals, televisions, movie screens and mannequins. His next? A mansion that was an amusement park and a shelter for children: a Disney-like property with its proper constituency. He placed himself at the center of this universe as the only human who was also a mythical creature, the missing link (but elevated, not degraded) between humans and animals, grown-ups and children, real life and fairy tales.

Follow me from a master builder of popular culture to some of its star performers. Michael put together his own legacy. He revered the black forerunners: James Brown, Jackie Wilson, Diana Ross, Sammy Davis Jr. If his white forerunners were Hollywood stars of an older generation, he revered them too. But if they were rock and pop stars, they had to be dealt with differently. They'd gotten all the props and the perks. They'd been crowned the prime movers, the brainy creators, the ones with the depth, the flash and the vision.

Elvis the King. Heavy hangs the head that wears the crown, true. But lucky and blessed is the man the world crowns king. If you have to claim it for yourself—if you feel you're from a family, a tribe, a clan denied its proper due—do what you have to do, but get that crown. The old Negro spiritual says "all God's chillun got crowns." Not in this world they don't—certainly not the Negroes who made the spirituals. White America made Elvis the King of Rock and Roll. (Yes, he had black fans, too, but they didn't count with the power brokers.) All the culture's resources were there for him. The big-time *Billboard* and *Variety* pop charts, not the provinces of "race music" or "rhythm and blues." The royal road to movie stardom: sex appeal that went from bad boy across the tracks to good boy next door. Hot moves, a sexy voice and a tender reverence for the Lord's gospel music too. Talent? Deluxe voice? Charisma? You bet.

Kings are supposed to compete with their predecessors and kings are supposed to marry other royals. Elvis's widow, Priscilla Presley, makes clear that she saw Michael Jackson as a scheming pretender, building Neverland to top Graceland, then courting Elvis's daughter to secure his lineage. But why shouldn't Lisa Marie Presley want the only man in the world as famous and powerful as her father? A man who might help her find her own way as a singer-songwriter, yet keep her in the royal arena to which she was accustomed?

As for The Beatles, why are they here? Didn't John Lennon say The Beatles were bigger than Jesus? Michael learned to be as big as The Beatles. He learned to be bigger when he outbid Paul McCartney and purchased the Beatles' catalog (a clever twist on the old money, power and race equation that had white performers outselling black ones with cover versions of black hits). And Michael, too, tried to make himself bigger than Jesus: in the *Brace Yourself* video of 1995 he is an enormous stone statue flanked by armies, come to save the world from the sins of war and inhumanity, come to halt the devastation of the planet, come to rescue innocent victims and children.

But look, here's an entertainer with no name, just another show-business trouper. She knew her stuff though. Michael saw her at the Apollo Theater in the early 1960s, when he and his brothers were still on the chitlin' circuit. He never forgot her.

> I had seen quite a few strippers, but that night this one girl with gorgeous eyelashes and long hair came out and did her routine. She put on a *great* performance. All of a sudden, at the end, she took off her wig, pulled a pair of big

oranges out of her bra, and revealed that she was a hard-faced guy under all that makeup. That blew me away. I was only a child and couldn't even conceive of anything like that. But I looked out at the theater audience and they were *going* for it, applauding wildly and cheering. I'm just a little kid, standing in the wings, watching this crazy stuff.

I was blown away.[7]

What a moment: blown away, swept away to someplace else. Children work so hard at learning what's expected of them, what grown-ups want from them. Or what grown-ups say they want. Kids learn by mimicking adult behavior and following adult instructions. If you think a gender switch shocking, try making sense of what some parents do versus what they say.

So, to be young, gifted and a witness to an act that violates all models of adult behavior in your life might be scary, but it's a thrill too. "Life ain't so bad at all, if you live it off the wall." A transvestite is like a cartoon. It keeps changing shape. It breaks the rules of cause and effect. It excites and incites the audience. A transvestite crosses gender zones. A transvestite masters the art of the betwixt and between. A transvestite works against nature, fights off time. But who wants to see an aging transvestite? Who wants to see an aging star, for that matter, especially a female whose face (worked over too much or not enough) has become a freak version of its younger self? It's no wonder that Michael Jackson has been compared to Gloria Swanson in *Sunset Blvd.*: to Norma Desmond, a travesty looking very much like an aging transvestite, a freak.

Little freak, who made you? Dost thou know who made you? Genes made you. Disease and illness made you. Religion made you. Show business and science made you. History made you: the norms and needs of your time and place made you. Your family and your psyche made you.

Home

"Home is the place where, when you have to go there, / They have to take you in." In a way these lines by Robert Frost can be quite terrifying. There you are, blood kin, shut up together—immured—in the place you fought so hard to leave behind. What won't you do to punish one another this time around? The Jacksons are a scary family. They've been a public-relations construct and a myth in progress from the start: the up-from-nothing family; the show-business family; the black-family-values family and now the "Hollywood Scandals" and "Fame Is a Bitch" family. Their story is a tale told by journalists, scriptwriters, fans and a cast of ex-employees, from lawyers and managers to gardeners and valets.

A family can be like organized religion: just about any crime can be committed and hidden in its name, and the Jacksons have plenty to answer for. Start with its lethally Victorian structure. Joseph Jackson, the patriarch, who will *make* his children learn the hard lessons of obedience and survival. Katherine, the soft-voiced mother, constantly tends to her children's physical and spiritual needs. Joseph and Katherine work hard every day. They have nine mouths to feed, nine children to shepherd through school and shield from bad influences. Everyone is up at dawn. Everyone has chores to do. No one is allowed to play with other kids except at school, where contact cannot be avoided.[1]

Joseph works in a steel mill. When times are very tight, he digs potatoes. But somehow he always finds time for sexual dalliances. Katherine works at home, caring for all their children. When money gets very tight, she works at Sears part-time. Katherine's three youngest children are between the ages of six and two; Michael is five. She has time for nothing else until that day in 1963 when a Jehovah's Witness rings her doorbell. Politely but firmly, the worker speaks about the dangers of this world and the rewards of the next.

"Good morning. I have come to bring you good news about a perfect new world without crime. Wouldn't you like to live in a world where you didn't have to lock your doors, and where all creatures lived under the law and order of a perfect ruler?

"I am bringing all your neighbors a message of comfort and hope from the Bible. I see that you have a little child. Wouldn't you like him to grow up in a world where there was no sickness and no death?"

The worker leaves literature for Katherine to study, a copy of *The Watchtower* or *Awake!* or the *Witness Truth* book, "Dedicated to Jehovah and to Jesus Christ." That same year Katherine is baptized in the swimming pool of Roosevelt High School (soon to become famous as the alma mater of Jackie, Tito and Jermaine, and the site of The Jackson Five's first talent contest win).

As it turns out, the Witnesses might have done better to ask Katherine such questions as: Wouldn't you like to be rich? Wouldn't you like to have a mansion in sunny California called Hayvenhurst framed by Tivoli lights instead of this tiny clapboard house in a poor Gary neighborhood where you all crowd into the kitchen to warm yourselves before the oven on cold winter nights? Wouldn't you like your boys to be world-famous and celebrate you with words like these from the liner notes of *Destiny:* "A mother is a gift given from God. For ours we are most grateful, and we dedicate this album to our beautiful mother, Katherine Jackson."

For the time being, the Witnesses give Katherine Jackson a way to live with what she lacks as she struggles to support her family and get her high school equivalency degree: money, friends and a husband who is kind and faithful. Joseph Jackson did not become a Witness, nor did he stop abusing his children. But Katherine would turn the pain and sacrifice of her life into a promise of salvation.

Jehovah's Witness theology deems the world a vile and evil place where God and Satan do constant battle for the souls of mankind. Eons ago Satan boasted that he could turn men away from God. Job was the test case, so God obviously won. But He craves perpetual vindication and therefore "restrains himself" from putting an end to evil. This is for our own good, for how else can mankind learn to uphold Jehovah as "rightful Sovereign and One deserving to be feared and worshipped." On the glorious day that the world ends and Satan's reign collapses, legions of evildoers will be cast into hell's abyss. Two classes of worshippers will be saved. The second-class ones will have everlasting life on a newly cleansed earth. The first-class ones, 144,000 in number, will serve with Christ in heaven as corulers and associate kings.

Women form more than half the Witnesses' membership, and they do most of the door-to-door proselytizing. Yet they do not hold leadership positions because Charles Taze Russell, who founded the Zion's Watchtower Bible and Tract Society in 1884, decreed: "Strength of mind and body by divine arrangement abides with, and constitutes man the head of the family . . . it is for the husband to weigh, to consider, to balance, to decide." Like so many born to be subordinate, women did not always accept their natural state. They easily grew "depraved and selfish," inclined to "usurp the authority of the head of the home, to take and to hold the control of the purse and of the family . . ." A good woman's qualities should be "an expression of the man's honor and dignity." (It should be noted that Russell's wife, Maria, who helped edit the organization's journal, left him after eighteen years of marriage, filing for separation on grounds of cruelty and infidelity.) Ex–Jehovah's Witness Barbara Grizzuti Harrison wrote: "As a child, I observed that it was not extraordinary for women who became Jehovah's Witnesses to remove themselves from their husbands' bedrooms as a first step to getting closer to God. Many unhappily married and sexually embittered women fall in love with Jehovah."[2]

Katherine Jackson had turned her back on Baptist and Lutheran churches when she found out that their ministers were having extramarital affairs. Now her husband was doing the same, and under those circumstances you had better find a way to turn what you must bear into what you can and should bear, especially if you have sworn to stay in your marriage at all costs because you grew up in a broken home. The worst thing about endless duty and sacrifice is the anonymity. All poor, unhappy people aren't alike, but they often look alike to the outside world, and they know it. Katherine's new faith was a balm. Barbara

Grizzuti Harrison again: "Witness women feel that they *count*. Even their pain is valuable to them; their pains are the arrows of God. . . . Their religion enables them to make sense of the world—the world where people don't 'behave right,' where people do one another wrong."

Katherine Jackson's pursuit of her faith was analogous to what she had been doing all along: housekeeping. Dirt and disorder were the enduring enemy in the household. Germ-free spiritual cleanliness was the goal in her religion. The Witnesses say you are not pure in heart unless you are pure in body. You *must* follow scriptural condemnation of fornicators, idolaters, masturbators, adulterers and homosexuals. (Biblical citations are always provided.) Sinful conduct can lead to excommunication, called "dis-fellowshipping." "The believing woman is told that she may be the instrument of her husband's salvation. . . . She cannot but feel superior to the man who is scheduled for destruction, while at the same time she must act as if the man who despises or is indifferent to her beloved Jehovah is, by Divine arrangement, the head of her household."

Now let us turn to Joseph Jackson, the man who stopped at nothing to maintain his position as head of the household. His daughter La Toya's memoir gives the only hint of his youthful appeal. He did attract women long before he had money, even though in most recent photographs he bears a fearsome resemblance to Blacula, the African-American vampire played by William Marshall in the 1972 movie. What La Toya calls the "sexy smile" of his youth will have become a sneer by the time his sons are famous, the "sharply arched eyebrows" villainous. She's right about the reddish hair and emerald eyes: they would definitely have made him a catch. (Katherine was his second wife, and his flings were numerous.)

Joseph Jackson has often been called a "strict disciplinarian"—a Victorian euphemism in light of J. Randy Taraborrelli's interviews with the Jacksons and their relatives, La Toya's revelations ("Here is my book, the one my family doesn't want you to read"), Michael's public statements and Joseph's crude rebuttals. "I whipped him with a switch and a belt. I never beat him. You beat someone with a stick."

There's a freaky *Till Eulenspiegel* quality to some of the abuse. He put on ghoulish masks and scared his children awake, tapping on their bedroom window, pretending to break in and standing over their beds, waiting for them to wake up screaming. This adds a new dimension to the monsters in the haunted mansion of *Thriller.* And to the doubles who keep popping up in Michael's video cosmology: good Michael/demon Michael; Michael the savior/Michael the killer (though he kills to save the innocent); Michael who sings in a song called "Threatened": "You're fearing me 'cause you know I'm a beast / Watchin you while you sleep."

Joseph was the martinet rehearsal captain. When one of the boys missed a dance step, he got whipped— and mocked, and scornfully compared to whichever brothers hadn't messed up. Where was Katherine when this was going on? In the background, looking sad; in the foreground, trying to placate; slipping in afterward to attend to the beaten child's hurt.

You have to go into a social-psychology mode to feel at all sympathetic toward Joseph Jackson. His father, Samuel, was a high school teacher, which would have been ultrarespectable in the Fountain Hills, Arkansas, of the 1930s. His second wife was one of his students, and Joseph was the oldest of their five children. When Joseph was a teenager, they divorced. Joseph went to California with his father, while the other children went with their mother, Chrystal, to East Chicago. When Samuel acquired a third wife, Joseph returned with him to East Chicago and managed to drop out of high school soon afterward. What better punishment for the strict, education-minded paterfamilias who, as Joseph recalled years later, "treated me like one of his students, not like a son"? Joseph always knew how to hit people where it hurt most, then claim (and believe) it was for their own good. He admired his father's child-rearing methods, he insisted in interviews. Children *should* fear their parents more. Strictness had been good for him. And hadn't he made sure it was good for his sons? Look at what they'd achieved.

But what exactly had Joseph himself achieved? Never what he most desired. After dropping out of high school, he became a Golden Gloves boxer—but never a champion like Jackie Wilson or a steady winner like Berry Gordy. He did not become a successful musician or producer, either. But he loved music and longed to break into the business, so he put his own R & B band together. The Falcons played local clubs and colleges, covering the hits of Chuck Berry, Little Richard, Otis Redding and such. Were they exceptional? No. Were they successful? No. This is the moment when Joseph becomes poignant. He wanted it so much and he tried so hard to get it.

Now look at Joseph's guitar, sitting in the bedroom closet at 2300 Jackson Street. In one version of what follows, The Falcons have already disbanded; in another they're struggling on with failure in plain sight. In whatever version, Joe forbids his sons to *ever* touch that instrument. Sometimes, though, Katherine—who can also play piano and clarinet—takes it out and serenades her children with the country songs she loves and once dreamed of performing onstage. They sing along on "The Great Speckled Bird" and "Wabash Cannonball." But what the kids are really crazy about is the new soul music on the radio. Soon they're sneaking into the bedroom on their own to pick out tunes on Daddy's guitar and sing together. One day Tito, who looks just like his father and has been studying guitar at school, breaks a string. The Oedipal moment has arrived. A furious Joseph strikes his second son; Tito runs to his room and falls on the bed crying.

Michael remembers Joseph's entering the room and ordering Tito to stand. Giving him "a hard pene-trating look," he issues the classic R & B challenge: "Let me see what you can do." Tito remembers saying: "You know, I can play that thing. I really can." To which Joseph replies in classic bully style, "Okay, lemme see what you can do, smart guy." La Toya remembers Katherine rushing to Joseph's side, pleading her son's case. Be that as it may, Tito did play, Jackie and Jer-maine began to sing along and Joseph saw that his dream could be—and would have to be—lived out by proxy.

So while Katherine works to lead their souls to God, Joseph works to bend their minds, bodies and voices to his will for success. Not that Katherine objects: she has her own suppressed ambitions. The boys become singing and dancing machines. And little Michael becomes a diligent Witness. In one of his many testimonials to Katherine, he writes: "Despite all the time we spent rehearsing and traveling, Mom would find time to take me to the Kingdom Hall of the Jehovah's Witnesses, usually with Rebbie and La Toya."

Those words "Mom would find time" bother me. They imply yet another act of maternal selflessness: whatever the hour, whatever the time, Mom would put her son's needs first. But Katherine wasn't the one constantly rehearsing and traveling; Michael was. She wasn't "finding time" to take her spiritually needy son to the Kingdom Hall; she was making sure that he went there with her, stayed by her side and became one of the faithful. Faithful to the church and faithful to Mother.

Religious sects proselytize. So do mothers when they are in a bad marriage with no way out. It's their only sure weapon. They try to convert the children to their emotional cause—to win their abject love and loyalty. Every bit of pain, every setback, becomes proof of Katherine's goodness, her capacity for sacrifice. The polio that had left her with a limp and without the music career she longed for? "My mother knew that her polio was not a curse but a test that God gave her to triumph over, and she instilled in me a love of Him that I will always have."

Her sons all agreed that their musical talent came from their mother. They weren't sure about the dancing, but Katherine let them know this much: it sure didn't come from Joseph, whom, La Toya records, she always told, " 'You can't even keep a beat.' It's true. He snaps his fingers or claps his hands to music, but off the beat." Oh yes, Katherine found little ways of getting her own back, at least momentarily. And apparently she also found ways to give her children a sense of being loved.

In one of those deft underhanded jibes Michael regularly directs at Joseph, he gives Katherine the kind of praise one usually gives the father who has worked long hours at several grueling jobs to support his family: "There isn't one of us who's ever forgotten what a hard worker and a great provider she was." He means cooking, cleaning, sewing their clothes. But he's pointedly setting up an alternative to Joseph, who turned the home into a 24/7 sweatshop. When you think about the rehearsal schedule for the boys and the home tasks for the girls, you start to feel child labor laws ought to be enforced in the home.

When Michael describes how the children saw Katherine, we are back in the nineteenth century, where the only way a mother can temper her husband's brute force is through gentle influence. Katherine gave her children "the gift of love," constant examples of "kindness, consideration" and lessons in moral behavior. "Don't hurt people. Give but never beg. I wish we could all be more like Mom."

What's touching about these generically pious words is how desperate children are to find a savior—

or at least a comforter they can turn into a savior—in a home ruled by a tyrant. But Katherine also gives her children moments of real pleasure. It's there in her guitar playing and singing. La Toya remembers being beautifully dressed and fussed over. And Michael says she always tried to encourage their hobbies. His, anyway. "If I developed an interest in movie stars, for instance, she'd come home with an armful of books about famous stars . . ." Little did she know that one day some of them would usurp her position and become surrogate mothers.

La Toya was the first Jackson child to expose Joe's physical abuse, but Michael is a master at passive-aggressive paternal payback. He has his own way of dealing blows that leave no obvious marks. He says his mother always taught him that talent was a gift from God: "What I got from my father wasn't necessarily God-given, though the Bible says you reap what you sow." Ostensibly Michael is talking about his father's lectures on hard work, planning and preparation. But the biblical warning gives the sentence an ominous turn. Michael got slaps, hard words and lessons in cruelty from his father. Joseph had better get ready for the Big Payback.

But overall his preferred voice suggests: "I'm too good a person to be cruel or try to get even. I have to tell the truth . . . but I'll be as forgiving as I can." He writes, "My father did always protect us and that's no small feat ... He might have made a few mistakes along the way, but he always thought he was doing what was right for his family." (Translation: My father did manage the baseline duties. Not as well as he thinks, of course, but he did the best he could, given his limitations, which I'm too good a son to enumerate.)

What a setup! Joseph is placed in an infamous gallery of parents: scoundrels, like Jackie Coogan's mother and stepfather, whose outrageous cheating led the state of California to pass child income protection laws. In that context he's not so bad. "He looked out for both our interests and his." Then comes the body blow: "But I still don't know him, and that's sad for a son who hungers to understand his own father." He didn't steal money. He stole Michael's birthright: a father's love.

Joseph and Katherine Jackson pushed five sons to stardom and one to superstardom. They also created a group of emotionally dependent adults with damaged egos. Years of sibling and professional rivalry had to be suppressed onstage and denied offstage. And except for Michael, none of the brothers could manage to leave home except by marrying.

Here is the body count ...

Jackie (Sigmund Esco): The eldest brother, the one (according to La Toya) most scorned by Joseph and least protected by Katherine. Jackie turned out to

41

be the family's talent scout. He decided that five-year-old Michael should be the lead singer, displacing Jermaine. Jackie thrived on the sexual perks of fame: he was eighteen when The J-5 became matinee idols. He remained passive for the next fifteen years: following orders to be blandly upbeat with the press, saying nothing Motown publicists had not approved in advance.

Tito (Toriano Adaryll): Brother number two looked so much like Joseph Jackson that Michael says almost nothing about him in *Moonwalk* beyond "the extent of the resemblance was scary as he got older." Tito had begun it all by stepping up and playing his father's broken guitar. And Tito was the first to be made functionally useless once the boys reached Motown. What need did their crack studio band have for his modest skills? He wasn't always allowed to record background vocals, either. But he could sing and play on tours, and he could hold the guitar in his arms on album covers. It's like what Phil Spector told Bobby Hatfield, the lesser Righteous Brother, who complained that all he'd be singing on "You've Lost That Loving Feeling" was the refrain. (The tale comes from Cynthia Weil, who wrote the hit with Spector and Barry Mann.) "What am I supposed to do the rest of the time?" Hatfield demanded. "Go to the bank and count your money," came Spector's crisp reply.

Jermaine Lajuane: The third brother thrice denied his chance—his *right*, as he sees it—to be a star: by his own brother, by his father, and by his boss and father-in-law, Berry Gordy Jr., founder of Motown. Jermaine was the piss-and-vinegar kid, the joker (like Michael), ambitious (like Michael) and the only one Michael called "a big brother to me." It was Jermaine who walked him to kindergarten, Jermaine whose hand-me-down clothes he wore. (Hand-me-downs can give an admiring younger sibling quite a thrill.) Jermaine was the brother Michael watched as a fledgling performer. When the Jacksons left Motown and Jermaine decided to stay, Michael was desolate. From those first rehearsals in that cramped Gary living room, Jermaine had been at Michael's left, playing bass ("I *depended* on being next to Jermaine"). But, as Michael carefully adds, on the night when Jermaine announced his departure from the group and left before the second show, the remaining brothers went back onstage and got not one, not two but three standing ovations. Jermaine was to have neither a happy marriage nor a well-run solo career. He came to see Michael's eventual triumph as a betrayal. And he learned to play Judas. Jermaine was the one who threw out an angry (and opportunistic) challenge to Michael's mutating looks with his song "Word to the Badd!" in 1991. Knowing Michael had not one but two sons named Prince Michael, Jermaine would trump him (upping the ante on black nomenclature) by christening his son Jermajesty. It was Jermaine who allegedly confided to a "close associate" who confided to the *National Enquirer* that he—and his family—all believed Michael was guilty of pedophilia. Jermaine denied it.

Marlon David: It is not a happy fate, in the Jackson family, to be a year older than Michael Jackson without his talent. Like Elvis and Liberace, Marlon had a twin who did not survive infancy. But Marlon did not, like them, become star enough for two. Marlon has the sweetest, saddest face in group photos. But Marlon also has the keenest sense (after Michael) of how to pose for a camera. La Toya claims he had the hardest time learning the choreography, got the most beatings from Joseph and practiced the hardest. La Toya also has Katherine correcting Marlon's emotions as sternly as Joseph did his moves. Asked by Jackie why she was so hard on Marlon, she supposedly answered: "Because he can't be so competitive, Jackie. It's a bad trait and he's got to break himself of it before he gets older." It must be said that La Toya's recall is too absolute and too self-serving to be altogether credible. But the duty, piety and psychological obtuseness sound like Katherine. Some of La Toya's major charges were verified (after initial family denials). Damaged children of fame, from La Toya to Christina Crawford, do tell certain truths—factual and emotional—despite all their exaggerations and the all-too-clear signs of their psychic damage.

Randy (Steven Randall): The youngest. He joined the group when Jermaine left, filling Michael's original place as the little fellow on the bongos. Randy is the shadow brother. It's as if his elders sucked all the oxygen out of him, while Janet was busy scrambling for the rewards of being the baby. Randy does show up when things get violent, though. In 1980, when he was eighteen and Janet fourteen, they were charged with helping Katherine beat up a woman she believed to be Joseph's current mistress. Later that year he almost lost both legs in a car accident (he was driving). Ten years later his wife filed for divorce: Randy, she said, had beaten her throughout her pregnancy. Convicted of spousal abuse, Randy spent one month in prison and one month in a psychiatric facility.

Rebbie (Maureen Reilette): The eldest and prettiest Jackson, Rebbie spends her youth as a mother's aide: the quiet daughter we know so well from Victorian life who disappears into homemaking and churchgoing. She does know certain family secrets: it is Rebbie who tells a family friend that when Michael was a teenager, "someone he trusted" decided that his sexual initiation was long overdue and had him "worked over" by three prostitutes. Rebbie did harbor show-business dreams.

45

In the midseventies, she, La Toya and Janet decided to go on the road with a sister act, but they couldn't agree on the group's direction. Anyway, Rebbie was in her mid-twenties by then, with no experience beyond token appearances on her brothers' television show. When the plan fell apart, she seemed to retreat into the family once more. In 1984 her debut album quickly and quietly tanked. But she has released six more in Japan.

La Toya Yvonne: La Toya was her mother's sheltered helpmate and "best friend." She was pretty, too, and for years she was a faithful, sexually pure Jehovah's Witness. Then, in the 1980s, she burst upon the world as pop culture's Madwoman in the Attic. First she recorded albums that didn't sell. Then she did a *Playboy* centerfold, complete with boa constrictor, that appalled her family and generated welcome media coverage. Soon she was appearing on *Solid Gold* and touring army bases with Bob Hope—extracting a minor career from minimal talent and good looks distorted by plastic surgery. Of course a couple of the brothers were less good-looking and hardly more gifted. With her love of flash and a certain spunk, if she'd gotten training and experience early, La Toya might have had a perfectly decent girl-group career. Instead she tried to burn down the family house by writing an autobiography called, with diva entitlement, *La Toya*. She certainly revealed some major structural damage there. As for the details: Did Joseph and Katherine really try to kidnap her? Did Michael offer a long, psychologically astute analysis of how her *Playboy* spread, like his *Thriller,* was a rebellion against a cruel father and a repressive religious upbringing? Everyone but La Toya says no. At this point I suspect that no one, including La Toya, knows for sure.

Janet Damita Jo: The baby girl with a middle name lifted from an expansively sultry black singer of the fifties and early sixties. Janet was lucky to be born in the late 1960s: time and history were on her side. When she was seven and the Jacksons were looking to conquer Las Vegas, Joseph saw her as a useful novelty in their act. That's how she got to sashay onstage in a feather boa doing a Mae West imitation. Then she got in on the black TV comedy boom. Her roles on *Good Times* (*"Dy-no-miiiite!"*) and *Diff'rent Strokes* made her not a star but a savvy little professional. Janet chafed at family dictates about a girl's place in the home and the world. By the time she fled home for a sleek young man with good hair and bad habits (James DeBarge of Motown, who had a drug problem), she was in full rebellion. By the time they divorced, her ambition was in place. Like big sister La Toya, Janet had been recording non-hit albums under Joseph's guidance, but like many younger children she figured out how to oblige her family on the surface while dissenting behind their backs. She had watched Michael find his own producers; she did the same. She had seen him enhance and revise his looks; she did that, too, dieting, fiercely working out, and using surgery to reduce and enlarge various features and body parts. Onstage and in videos, she was choreographed to within an inch of her life. Without Janet there would have been no stardom for Paula Abdul, or Britney Spears. She was the original tiny-voiced teen girl rebel, the original hardest-working sex toy in show business.

Michael Joseph Jackson: Without him the others would hardly matter. A child prodigy makes life so hard for his siblings. He gets most of the attention without even trying. The others never stop trying; they're always struggling to find an identity that matters to others and themselves. If they manage, they must accept the fact that their hard-won identity may yield few rewards. Michael's brothers won money and fame, but not as individuals. They were always appendages or a unit. They had the usual sibling ways of getting back at Michael. Cruel nicknames ("Liver Lips" and "Big Nose"), the light bullying all older children have at their command, plus the right to set the general pace of daily life. This was especially true when it came to sex: Jackie, Tito and Jermaine flirted and fucked to their heart's content in plain sight of Michael. And he had ways to hold his own. He had his stockpile of nicknames ("Rocky Road" for a teenage Jermaine with acne; "Moonface" for little Janet's chubby cheeks and "Dunk" (from donkey) for her chubby behind). He was right at the center of the manic pranks—shaving cream fights, water balloons dropped from windows, room service meals delivered to strangers—that the brothers entertained themselves with when they were shut away for hours in hotels. He was gutsy, too, the only one, by most accounts, who stood up to Joseph's bullying. Michael was about five when he threw a shoe at his father while darting across the room to escape a beating. A few years later he told Joseph he'd stop singing if he ever got hit again. It seems the older brothers took their punishment, watched one another suffer in silence, then fussed when Joseph was safely gone. Talk about doing backup when your little brother is singing lead! Think of it. All those years of claustrophobic intimacy among the brothers in cars, dressing rooms and record studios, never more than a few inches or feet apart. There was no escape. And when they got to their Oz—Motown—the net widened and trapped them ever more securely. The brothers had moved from a nuclear family into a corporate one—traded a crude, domineering patriarch they had to please for a suave, domineering one they had to please and longed to impress. Having grown up in a small world of blood relations, they moved into the larger one of "bloods." Berry Gordy used race as the

Jacksons had used family. Never betray your blood or the bloods. Gordy always encouraged what we could euphemistically call creative competition. Everyone watched to see who had the most hits this month, who was being assigned the best writers and producers. Whom would Berry elevate next? Who would suffer benign neglect for a time, then be tossed out like worn equipment? Michael was the chosen one, the favorite child whom Gordy moved into Diana Ross's Hollywood home and crowded the rest of the family into a motel. Call this chapter in the life of The Jackson Four "They Were Expendable." Katherine had always claimed Michael was special. Diana felt—or was directed by Gordy to feel—the same. And as Michael had always depended on his mother to understand him and set the right example, he now looked to Diana to do the same. Morals and the nurturing of hobbies became manners and arts appreciation. No brother had anything more to teach him; he studied Diana's performance techniques. He anointed her his "mother, sister, lover," even as Motown helped him to begin the journey of ridding himself of his father: Gordy had brought Joseph down to size.

By 1977, nineteen-year-old Michael had shed the J-5 globular Afro. Short hair emphasized his wide eyes and slender limbs; the word "faunlike" was not inappropriate. He wore white and silver glitter jumpsuits to celebrate the rites of disco. But like a child at Halloween, what he loved best was hiding inside the clown clothes and red, plum-sized nose of The Scarecrow in *The Wiz*. It served notice to the world that Michael could hold his own as a star.

But the 1978 film, produced by Berry Gordy and directed by Sidney Lumet, was a lumbering flop. As Dorothy, Diana Ross was arch, bland, too thin and too old. Michael's performance is hurt by the film's torpor. His awkward, insecure Scarecrow is a real character, though, not a collection of bits. Like Ray Bolger in the original, he lets his body tell the tale. His limbs cross and fold as he learns to walk, then dance, with stumbling grace. He trips in his long shoes and rights himself, wavering. Despite his soft monotone, there are hints of merriment. Like Bolger, he is boyish. But Bolger's Scarecrow was goofy. Michael's Scarecrow is a melancholic.

We first see him stuck on his pole, mocked and bullied by crows, begging to be taken down. Each time the crows refuse, he pulls a slip of paper from his straw and reads the words of some philosopher aloud— pleadingly or stoically. He sings "You Can't Win," with rough, gospel edges of desperation. The torment feels genuine. It's a painful scene.

Once Michael was no longer a child, he would construct his own various families according to particular and exacting specifications. First he brought together exotic animals, cartoon figures and mannequins. Then, for parental and sibling figures to replace the tarnished ones he'd grown up with: Sammy Davis Jr., Fred Astaire, Jane Fonda, Liza Minnelli, Katharine Hepburn, Elizabeth Taylor—every one of them a lost boy or girl, ripped untimely from a normal childhood by stardom or family tragedy. Then, he went from kitsch and celebrity to flesh-and-blood children. The famous were first: Emmanuel Lewis and Macaulay Culkin in their prime. The unknown followed: the sick, the helpless, the needy, coming to Neverland to frolic and be fed. He would be mother and father, a miracle worker. He would do at Neverland what ordinary parents *should* but would or could not do for their children. Or so he imagined. He crowned himself the King of Pop and arranged two marriages. First he announced his nuptials with Lisa Marie Presley, daughter of the King of Rock and Roll. When she fled the royal palace eighteen months or so later, he wed Debbie Rowe, nurse to his plastic surgeon. Soon he could proudly announce the advent of two children, Prince Michael Joseph I and Paris Michael Katherine, most likely through in vitro fertilization. Debbie Rowe was dismissed. A few years later he claimed to have sired a third child, Prince Michael Joseph II, mother and means unknown.

Star Child

"We call contrary to nature what happens contrary to custom," Montaigne writes in his essay "On a Monstrous Child." So call this chapter the story of a boy who grew up outside of nature and custom: a boy named Michael Jackson. Seventh of nine children from a scrappy working-class family in the 1950s Midwest. A boy who's a man now, but not really. There is nothing natural about the making of child stars. They are little archaeological sites, carrying layers of show-business history inside them, fragments of history and tradition. Michael is clearly proud of this. Note the touch of disdain when he writes: "Some musicians— Springsteen and U2, for example—may feel they got their education from the streets. I'm a performer at heart. I got mine from the stage."

In the culture of show business, the child star is

required to turn all complications of age, race or sex into pure entertainment. To put Michael Jackson and his family in their proper setting, we need to go back—way back—to a time when "Jim Crow" was a song-and-dance routine, not a system of de facto and de jure segregation. Blackface minstrelsy gave white Americans their first experience of staged Negro dance, music and talk, along with some of its first child stars. In the 1830s, as the form swept the country, five-year-old Joseph Jefferson toured with white minstrelsy's founding father, Thomas "Daddy" Rice. The little boy would tumble out of a valise, dressed just like Daddy in red-and-white-striped pants and a blue cutaway with gold buttons. The pair would sing "Jump Jim Crow" in dialect, then wheel, turn, jump and "set the heel a-rockin' " as they landed. They'd end by tossing their coat buttons, actually five- and ten-dollar gold pieces, to a rapturous crowd.

Though the "Jump Jim Crow" number was lifted from an old black man entertaining himself behind a livery stable, Negro children with an uncanny gift for song and dance were first glimpsed doing similar routines on streets and plantations as seen in nineteenth-century fiction and travel writing. *Uncle Tom's Cabin* gave these children pop culture immortality in 1852. In the novel's first chapter readers met their first pickaninny: he was pretty little Harry, son of the mulatto slaves Eliza and George. At his master's command, Harry sings, dances and mimics a lame old Negro. His master tosses him nuts and raisins, and a visiting slave trader promptly offers to buy him.

Emancipation freed the black boy-child to go into show business. By the 1870s all-male black minstrel troupes were touring the country. (Most women would have to wait until the 1890s.) Pickaninnies became theater "picks": well-crafted ornaments for adult entertainment. White *Uncle Tom's Cabin* troupes hired them for lavish plantation song-and-dance scenes. Black companies had whole brass bands of them. Boy sopranos who could warble spirituals and Stephen Foster tunes were separate but equally useful commodities.

By the early twentieth century, vaudeville's top white women were hiring pics to supply their acts with rhythmic pizzazz and knockout dance moves. Little black boys cakewalked, clogged in Dutch wigs, mimicked Russian steps and recycled dances from the black South as imports from Asia, Africa or the South Seas. There were fabulously precocious picks like little Bill "Bojangles" Robinson. There were serviceable chorus picks, too, never destined for solo fame. Like The Jackson Five minus Michael.[1]

Some children are born into show-business families; some leave their families behind to enter show business. Either way, only the rare and lucky ones have sensible parents who are reasonably satisfied with their own lives. The many less fortunate have parents who need the money and crave the reflected glory but still resent being overshadowed by the children they have pushed onstage.

The Jackson Five did what their parents could not do. Mother Katherine had real musical talent and longed to be a country-and-western singer, an unlikely wish in the pre–Charley Pride era, especially since a bout of childhood polio left her with a noticeable limp. She had to settle for marrying a philanderer—a country-and-western cliché—and singing to nine children. Father Joseph, a welder and crane operator, with his own guitar and his own unsuccessful rhythm and blues band, had to settle for a dream deferred.

Michael Jackson was sealed into the world of show business by the age of five. He and his brothers rehearsed six hours a day: three before school, three after. They started out with the soul hits they were listening to on the radio. Joseph would study the dance moves of other groups and pass them on to his boys. From 1964 to 1968, the Jacksons toiled and toured such local clubs in Gary, Indiana, as the Guys and Gals Cocktail Lounge and recorded in such mammy-made recording studios as Steeltown and Dynamo. There were weekend trips to Chicago and New York for amateur contests at the big theaters with imperial names. The Regal. The World-Famous Apollo.

They slept piled in the backseat of a station wagon,

mouths open, heads on one another's shoulders; did their homework backstage and in motels. They were cut off from crime, poverty and obscurity—also from hobbies, friends and just goofing around. They won the amateur contests and got a spot on the bill with real pros: The Coasters, Etta James, Sam and Dave, The Temptations, Gladys Knight and The Pips. And Mr. Excitement, Jackie Wilson, and Mr. Dynamite, Mr. Please Please himself, James Brown. Children never forget the people who first embody the possibilities of adult glamour and mastery. Show-business children can't afford to forget: they're busy picking up tricks from them.

When Michael was too young to join the family act, he would watch Jermaine in fascination. Once he'd replaced him as lead singer, Michael would stand in the wings and watch every single act that came onstage: "I'd stare at their feet, the way they held their arms, the way they gripped a microphone, trying to decipher what they were doing and why they were doing it. After studying James Brown from the wings, I knew every step, every grunt, every spin and turn."

He constructed himself from the best of what he witnessed on the chitlin' circuit. But the genealogy of child stars is often peculiar. Michael's first public performance had been in kindergarten, when he thrilled the assembly with a rapturous version of "Climb Every

Mountain." He moved seamlessly from the Mother Superior's anthem of emotional uplift to the ecstatic vision of Jackie Wilson on the wall at the Apollo dressing room, "one leg up, twisted, but not out of position from catching the mike stand he'd just whipped back and forth." But then, Jackie Wilson had no trouble moving between "Doggin' Around" and "Danny Boy." Michael learned that soul music was shrewdly deployed passion: a rhythm of contained and released energy. Soul music was also the right stage effect, the visual detail that enhanced the vocals. Those gorgeous patent-leather shoes the singers wore. It's such a child's-eye view: Michael standing in the dusty wings of a theater, mesmerized by shiny shoes.

"My whole dream seemed to center on having a pair of patent-leather shoes. . . . I'd go from store to store looking for patent-leather shoes and they'd say, 'We don't make them that small.' I was so sad because I wanted to have shoes that looked the way those stage shoes looked, polished and shining, turning red and orange when the lights hit them. Oh, how I wanted some patent-leather shoes like the ones Jackie Wilson wore."

All children have a private culture put together from what they see and hear every day and from objects they turn into fetishes. It's a space to play and dream in. But Michael's private culture has always been turned into the stuff of his work life. Now it is the stuff of a private mythology that he lives by and that we struggle to grasp.

Child stars have to live out adult mythologies. They work for adults. They perform "youth" as scripted by adults and they work adult hours to do so. A close-up of The Jackson Five at a Gary nightclub in the late 1960s: "We were playing between bad comedians, cocktail organists and strippers . . . five sets a night, six nights a week—and if Dad could get us something out of town for the seventh night, he was going to do it." There's nothing the kids don't pick up on: gossip, competition, sex. What's the exact line between parent-protectors and parent-pimps? Adults as mentors and lovers? Fans as worshippers and predators? Here is Michael in a Chicago club, again in the late 1960s: "I must have been nine or ten. This girl would take off her clothes and her panties and throw them to the audience. The men would pick them up and sniff them and yell. My brothers and I would be watching all this, taking it in, and my father wouldn't mind."

Nothing charms grown-ups like seeing kids imitate them. Children make our needs and habits entertaining; they follow our scenarios. Who do we want them to be? Wounded innocent? Flirt? Vixen? Naughty little chip off the old block? They know how to do it but they can't know exactly why they're so alluring. They embody adult secrets, and that gives us the upper hand.

Sadism, circa 1900: Young Buster Keaton gets raves playing a miniature version of his father in the family vaudeville act. He stands behind Keaton Sr. in baggy pants, cutaway coat and a bald fright wig, mimicking every word and action and being rewarded with a kick. Or sometimes a suitcase handle is placed between his shoulders so that Dad can hurl him about the stage without tearing his clothes. Buster retaliates by thwacking Dad's skull with a basketball.[2]

Titillation, 1917: A four-year-old whippersnapper named Jackie Coogan bounces onto a stage in San Francisco and shakes his tiny body from head to toe. The Shimmy had been a hit in black burlesque for almost a decade, but little Jackie was a year ahead of the grown woman (Gilda Gray) who would make it a national craze in the *Ziegfeld Follies*.[3]

Race and gender freakishness, 1927: Two-year-old Sammy Davis Jr. joins his father (who calls *Sammy* "Poppa") in Will Mastin's touring company. He's put in blackface and dressed like Al Jolson for his first stage appearance. Then, seated in the leading lady's lap, he mimics Jolson's broad gestures while she sings Jolson's hit "Sonny Boy." So a black boy imitates a white man who imitates a black man singing to a black or white boy.[4]

Decadence, circa 1968: The Jackson Five are doing cover versions of soul hits at Mr. Lucky's, a funky nightspot in Gary. Michael knocks the crowd out with his variation on "Skinny Legs," a Joe Tex number that could pass for a minstrel routine. A very country-sounding Joe is loud-talking some poor woman who has to walk down the street exposing her meager limbs to any man who cares to look. Joe offers her to every man, but no one wants her. "Don't you worry about a doggone thang at all," he assures her as the chorus pounds in. "Because there's someone, somewhere" who'll take the sister, "skinny legs and all!" In Michael's playful version: "We'd start the song and somewhere in the middle I'd go out into the audience, crawl under the tables, and pull up the ladies' skirts to look under. People would throw money as I scurried by, and when I began to dance I'd scoop up all the dollars and coins that hit the floor earlier and push them into my pockets."

Michael has followed Sammy Davis Jr. on a downward path from precocity to stardom to revilement. But Sammy never had Michael's level of early success. The glamour of pop music and the grand reach of integration made Michael an international idol. He was the Shirley Temple of our day—the greatest child star in the world. His collection of Shirley memorabilia sug-

gests that he understands their bond very well. They both got into the business through precocious sex appeal. Shirley's first films were a series of "Baby Burlesk" shorts. Her roles included a strumpet on the payroll of The Nipple Trust ("Decked out in a black satin and lace gown created by Mother, I swayed stiff-legged up to the senator and cooed, 'Aw c'mon, Senator, you can be had' "), and a tough French barmaid who entertained the Yanks in "an off-the-shoulder blouse and trademark diaper, a giant rose perched over one ear." The first dictionary definition of "pedophilia" is "sexual desire encouraged in adults for children." That's desire, not crime. We are supposed to think of hard-core pornography. But who could watch Michael's performances or Shirley's movies (despite their sugary plots) without knowing that desire—deftly modulated, nicely sublimated—is being encouraged?

When it came to race, Shirley and Michael were cultural mulattoes. Shirley had the blond curls of Little Eva but with a wiry bounce. She had the fleet feet of Harriet Beecher Stowe's Topsy ("the blackest of her race"), while her dance partner and teacher, Bill Robinson, was a remastered Uncle Tom with rhythm instead of religion. Temple Black says that none other than D. W. Griffith proposed her partnership with the man she called Uncle Bo. Griffith understood Shirley's girl-woman allure. And nothing, he told MGM, excited the public like the pairing of a black man and a white

woman. Forty years later it would turn out that nothing excited the public like the sight of a little black boy impersonating a black man beguiling women of every race.

The Jacksons got to Motown Records just after Berry Gordy Jr. had triumphed in his quest to wed "The Sound of Young America" to the sound of young black America. When this empire-builder set out to market The Jackson Five, Papa Joe's years of coaching and touring receded. Their new life had begun, it was said, when the boys were spotted in a Gary theater by Diana Ross. Untrue: it was Gladys Knight who first urged Motown scouts to come see the act. But Gladys Knight looked like a buxom neighborhood girl. Gladys Knight hadn't been photographed for *Vogue.* Gladys Knight hadn't been playing Jennifer Jones to Berry Gordy's David O. Selznick. So Diana Ross became the designated benefactress of the five boys with bright smiles and globular Afros. Motown had become pop music's version of a Hollywood studio like MGM. Top production values. Crack studio players to back up—or hold up—the stars. A high gloss of gentility. The performers got diction and etiquette coaching. Their life stories were touched up, their public statements were rehearsed. The man at the top put his mark on everything and everybody. None

of the grimy dressing rooms, hair grease and late-night sweat of the chitlin' circuit clung to The Brothers. (It still clung to The Temps and to The Four Tops.) The Jackson Five looked sexually fresh and racially clean.

But I'm slipping into that tone—ironic, artfully dismissive—that Motown lures writers into when we crave cultural purity, the ineffable force of soul, the vision of brave rebels who forged rock and roll against heavy odds. We know too much about the manipulation behind the music. We get embarrassed by Motown's easy-access charm and its lack of southern-based soul. The integration strategy looks like a shameless bid for bourgeois respectability. That active seeking of a white audience always arouses shame—as if it must always signal ingratiation and self-hatred. Then we listen to its best songs—or just a lot of its good ones—and give in again. We yield to its shrewd, ebullient pleasures. And rightly so.

Motown was mass entertainment, like vaudeville or Tin Pan Alley. Mass entertainment is the will to please the many, even when the many are a few hundred folk crowding onto a showboat or circus ground. Entertainment feeds on, collects the particulars of folk life: ethnic talk, regional manners, social types. It broadens some, smooths out others. Then it fits them into genres we all know and trust: farce melodrama, stand-up comedy. The lively courtship song; the ballad about lost lovers or dear mothers; the sexy come-on

number. The folk love to see themselves on the main stage of the culture so long as they're not being ridiculed. The mass audience of non-folk gets fresh cultural excitement at low cost and low risk.

So of course Motown set out to woo black and white listeners. It set out to win young listeners, too, and draw a clear line between its black performers and those of the older generation. Age was always murky in the zone where rhythm and blues met rock and roll. The R & B voice gives off experience and authority. The thirty-something R & B men who moved to rock and roll jacked up the beat and played up youth energy. Chuck Berry wrote stories of teen life and added country-and-western amiability to his voice and arrangements. Little Richard sailed off into delirious though sexually charged nonsense poetry. Bo Diddley gave his tall-tale menace a hint of deadpan humor. Other black record labels had been cultivating the young folk. But Motown was better organized. It made Youth a special-interest group that it played up to relentlessly. Too relentlessly as time went on; too cynically and too safely. Motown was getting pretty long in the tooth when the Jacksons showed up in 1969.

The studio system was under strain. The balance between stars and contract players was off. Motown had always produced hits for two kinds of groups. In one, the lead singer's identity blended with the group's (Martha Reeves and The Vandellas, The Marvelettes,

The Temptations). In the other, the lead singer was clearly the star, as with The Miracles and The Supremes. (In the case of The Four Tops, the lead singer chewed up the scenery.) When it came to soloists, though, Motown was not a place that encouraged singers to do anything but follow orders. Marvin Gaye and Stevie Wonder fought to become songwriters and became rebels in the process. Diana Ross fought to become a superstar. With Gordy's support she made herself the measure—as singer and glamour girl—by which other women were found wanting. Mary Wells and Brenda Holloway withered in her shadow. Tammi Terrell died young. Gladys Knight plugged away until she could get a record deal somewhere else.

Think of Motown as music's version of great genre fiction. All the right elements were still in place when it started its decline. But the excitement—the new voice, the fresh twist—was fading away. When that happens, you see the genre's limits—what it won't allow—too plainly. The perfect Motown song didn't allow for emotional outbursts or improvisation. But it generated pure pleasure, addictive pleasure, and the Jacksons revived that. They were young and eager to produce classic Motown hits: a gleaming sound machine with every part in place. But they also had Michael, whose talent pushed the machine past its limits.

The Jackson Five brought youth culture back to

Motown. Let me qualify that: they brought a generation of new young fans to Motown and they charmed
some of the cynical old guard. They weren't exactly
youth culture as we defined it in 1969. By then "Young
America" was in an uproar. We who were young had
confrontation politics and more than one countercul-
ture. We had many kinds of music, too: soul, folk, acid
rock, funk; music for partying, for demonstrating and
for getting high. We would not have used The Jackson
Five except to party by: Motown made sure that nothing they said or did was political or even thoughtful.[5]

Between December of 1969 and September of 1970,
the Jacksons had four number-one hits. The first, "I
Want You Back," had been intended for Gladys Knight
and The Pips. It was filched and reworked into a
sparkling flyboy number. A flash of notes as the pianist
runs his fingers down the keys. Then the bass and guitar set an intensely rhythmic four-bar groove; drums
and piano reinforce it for another four bars, with
strings offering tactful melodic hints. Michael enters
(and it is the vocal equivalent of a star entrance) with a
wordless croon, holding a long, high vocal line as the
bass plucks out a low, crisp one, breaking it in the second measure with that soul testimony formula,
"Lemme tell you now."

He sings the opening line with brash confidence. "When I had you to myself you didn't want me
around . . ." That's just how we gripe when love and sex

go bad. But this is a child, and that gives the song a cheekiness it wouldn't otherwise have. He's singing for us, the foolish lovers; he sounds much more assured than we would and he's singing to us about things children aren't exactly supposed to know. Let no one demean the contributions of Jackie, Tito, Jermaine and Marlon. Their backup is deft and very satisfying: syncopated close harmonies that exhort ("un-uh-hunh") and affirm ("oooh-oooh"). They have their own falsettos (though Marlon's voice, like Michael's, has yet to change), but the older boys can trade low Sly Stone notes with the bass. That three of the five have men's voices heightens the sexual play.

The song builds to a fine soul finish, i.e., a well-planned emotional explosion. The boys start trading "All I want" and "All I need" and "Baby," alternating high and low voices, upping the pitch and the fervor with each refrain. On the last "one more chance," Michael punches out a "Hah" (an aggressive soul man "Hah!"), then a high "Oh!" followed by a higher (still raspy) "Oh!" He shouts one last "I want you back!" on a fadeout that suggests he will be carried reverently from the studio in a state of ecstatic collapse. All those years of watching James Brown have paid off.

Four men, including Berry Gordy, wrote most of the boys' hits. They called themselves The Corporation and turned a Sammy Davis midget joke into a sex ploy. In song after song Michael would be back in childhood

("When we played tag in grade school . . .") or use childish ways to romance girls ("Do-Re-Me / A-B-C / 1-2-3 / Baby you and me!": he shouts the last line out as if he's at a high school pep rally). There's an extended passage in "ABC" that I loved in 1970 and now find unnerving. It comes midsong, and it shows Motown imitating the heat of Stax-Volt. The band and the brothers groove behind Michael as he builds to a climax. The boy-to-man play gets rougher ("T-t-t-teacher's gonna show you how to get an A-aay," he taunts). Then, like one of those videos in which he suddenly becomes a werewolf, he turns into—well, it could be Otis Redding, Bobby Womack or Mr. Dynamite himself. He's chanting, "Shake your money-maker" (this is an eleven-year-old) with total sexual conviction. Then he adds a rough layer to his voice and shouts: "Sit down girl! I think I love you! / No! Get up girl! Show me what *you* can do!"

These hits made Michael a national sex object—a sex toy, really. And there was his dancing, of course. He was a little virtuoso with his Mr. Dynamite slides and kicks, the confident shoulder thrusts and outstretched arms of Mr. Excitement. All reinforced by the older brothers: their synchronized moves made clear that this was a flirting game.

Wherever they went, The Jackson Five were mobbed by fans and protected by guards. None of the boys had ever been protected from Joseph's philandering, though. Michael and Marlon weren't protected by their brothers, either: often they were in the hotel room when the guys brought back girls (some eager, some naïve) for bouts of star-prerogative sex. In 1971, Michael turned thirteen. What better advertisement of puberty's approach than to be on the cover of *Rolling Stone* and appear on Diana Ross's ABC special? In one skit he played a ghetto hustler: he talked like Shaft in his baby pipes voice, then swaggered off, leaving Diana flat. In another he did a Frank Sinatra parody. Leaning casually against a lamppost in fedora and trench coat, arm extended as if about to snap a casual finger, he filled "It Was a Very Good Year" with memories of sandboxes and school bells going "Ring-a-ding-ding."

My friends and I (graduate students all) found it precious and in no way peculiar. Why would we? We were dancing and dating to his love songs. And he'd become quite a suave little crooner. In "I'll Be There," the boyishness becomes a young lover's idealism. "Never Can Say Goodbye" is intense. That pure voice actually conveys emotions that smolder (anguish! doubt!) as it leaps up a sixth for the first vehement "Don't wanna let you go" and down a fourth for the closing one. In those early years of feminism, when few grown men seemed worth trusting, little Michael was our Cupid.

And, God, the outfits! The Jackson Five were youth

mascots and Motown tried to cover all youth bases. Ghetto glory, flower power, circuses, rock concerts, mod play, doo-wop glitter. The outfits were coordinated but never identical. The stage was a sartorial theme park. Jumpsuits, each in five or six different colors: tangerine, white and yellow pants with dark patches (the patches matched the boots); a shiny copper-colored belt; long-sleeved robin's-egg-blue top, the collar like a daisy; a copper neckband; fringe vests; berets and fedoras; bell-bottoms (always bell-bottoms) made from Indian blankets. Lift one leg and the fans see all green; lift the other leg, they see green up to the knee, then pink with maroon and white stripes on one side. In one photo they look like an op art quintet. Pants, belts, vests, shirts, every one in a different, very insistent pattern. And boots like spats, with broad white laces up to the knees. Berets, fedoras, apple caps, and the occasional cowboy hat.

What's amazing is how Michael adapts to each ensemble. He never looks silly or trapped in photos. Jackie, Tito and Jermaine often do; how can we blame them? He never looks shy, as Marlon does. Over and over we see the great performer's sense of body placement: how to use the camera or the stage frame. The turn of the shoulders, a slight crouch, a head tilt, an arm extended just so. As basketball players like to say: all the little necessities.

The Jackson Five didn't just move black performers closer to pop music's main stage, they moved black audiences there too. We talk a lot about black role models. Kids need teen idols just as much as they need role models—and they found them in Jackie, Tito, Jermaine, Marlon and Michael. Before rap, before hip-hop. The Jacksons ruled on both sides of the race aisle. You found them on the covers of black magazines ("The Jackson Five Are Taking Care of Business!"); you saw them on white TV shows (here's Ed Sullivan introducing "these fine young boys"); they had their own cartoon series. Once there had been a time when we read about white stars in *Life* and *Look* and black stars in *Ebony* and *Jet*. No more. There was nothing compensatory about The Jackson Five's popularity. You had an edge if you were a black fan—a slightly higher cool quotient—because they were black too.

The 1970s were an interesting decade for child performers. The culture was clearly obsessed—let's say "conflicted"—about children. Hardly surprising. Feminists and gays were upending the standardized vision of Man, Woman and Family. Children could hardly be left out. Little-girl movie stars made tattered childhoods attractively perverse. We got the manipulative pseudoadult without a mother (Tatum O'Neal in *Paper Moon*). The exquisitely decadent child prostitute without a mother (Brooke Shields in *Pretty Baby*). We got the jaded child with absent parents (Jodie Foster in *Alice Doesn't Live Here Anymore*) and the cynical child who serviced johns (Jodie Foster in *Taxi Driver*).

This may seem distant from The Jackson Five, but it is not distant from Michael. He was as much an object of sexual fantasies as any of these girls. The sexual precocity intensified as he sang ballads like "I'll Be There" and "Never Can Say Goodbye." So did our excited responses. The imp of the perverse showed up in 1973 when he appeared on the Academy Awards to sing "Ben," a slow, fervent pledge of love to a feral rat out to destroy a city. Michael had recorded it in 1972. It was a pure-voiced performance of great conviction. He was fourteen and it may be the most emotionally openhearted love song he has yet performed.

The Jackson Five had a huge effect on television. Producers desperately wanted to update family values with pop appeal. Who can forget watching the Osmonds change from sunny Mormon brothers who crooned with Andy Williams to boys in tight spangled pants who shook their groove things on *The Flip Wilson Show*? The press always portrayed the Jacksons as a tight-knit, loving family. Suddenly we had the tight-knit, loving Partridge Family as a white suburban pop band. The Jacksons made their way into white homes with their records and their ABC cartoon show. By the 1980s, black children were showing up in white television families. Is it any wonder that one of the first child friends Michael chose was Emmanuel Lewis, the tiny black star of *Webster*?

Here's the thing about Michael Jackson: he lives in extremis what other people have gone through—or fear or fantasize about. Michael began to talk publicly—almost compulsively—about his childhood ten years ago. The childhood that had been stripped from him: no birthdays, no Christmases, no happy memories of fun and play; only endless work and sacrifice. So it is that child stars are his chosen people: mentors, siblings and parents who give nothing but love and support. Elizabeth Taylor, Sammy Davis Jr., Fred Astaire. Tatum O'Neal and Brooke Shields—the only two women he ever suggested he was involved with romantically as an unmarried man. The damage suffered by child stars rarely shows by word or deed until they crash suddenly, leave the business or make their way to adult success. Then comes the anger, the grief, the cynicism and—the hardest of all—the longing for a prime you've been past for most of your life.

I've spent a lot of time with a book called *Twinkle Twinkle, Little Star: And Don't Have Sex or Take the*

Car by Dick Moore. Moore found fame in the 1930s as Dickie Moore, a little blond boy with huge eyes and a perfect bow-shaped mouth who went from Dietrich and Stanwyck dramas to *Our Gang* comedies. He talks intimately and very intelligently with child star veterans. And it's all here. Feeling used by every adult you know: "We were not working with peers but with directors, teachers, executives, agents, parents. As children, we were always the slaves. All these people had this goddamn age and experience over us and a certain ruthlessness that children do not have." Feeling responsible for every adult you know, too: "being driven to work in the morning as a child, feeling the kind of apprehension a man of forty would feel when he's on the Long Island Railroad to New York City, preparing to convince a meeting of the board that his next project is feasible" (Gene Reynolds). Knowing that you're being force-fed, that social and sexual rules are being stuffed down your gullet: Shirley Temple Black writes in her autobiography, *Child Star,* "It is not easy to be a Hollywood starlet. Starlets have to kiss a lot of people, including some unattractive ones. Often starlets are knocked down to the floor or pricked by their diaper pins. The hours are long. Some of the positions that must be assumed are downright uncomfortable ... Like a Girl Scout, starlets must be cheerful and obliging, particularly to directors, producers and cameramen. Like a Boy Scout, starlets must always be prepared, whether to recite lines, give a benefit performance or become the butt of a joke."

Celebrity demands a certain degree of hypocrisy from all performers. The persona can't possibly square with the private life. But it's much freakier for kids. Some of their fans are old enough to be their parents or grandparents. Fans their age are remote and frightening. They're not peers, they're worshippers who can decide to reject you at any time and find another idol. When it comes to gender roles, child stars do double duty. They are the man of the family: the provider, the financial mainstay. And they are the woman, too: the aesthetic and sexual object who *must* remain young and charming. Moore writes that when groups of child stars convene to share experiences, it can feel like a meeting of Alcoholics Anonymous. One can see why. But are they recovering children or recovering adults?

Even now Michael's voice is the voice of a sweet boy, a winning boy, a boy who never says anything ugly or unkind. A boy-angel child. A boy as good as Harriet Beecher Stowe's Little Eva. Listen to Janet's "baby-of-the-family voice," the whispery voice of the little thing who always got a big laugh when she sashayed out to do her Mae West imitation. Whenever they do something provocative—Janet's breast baring, Michael's

Thriller video—they disavow all knowledge of their own actions. Then they apologize for offending anyone: that was not their intention. Even the unsuccessful Jacksons bear the mark of regression. Watch Jermaine in interviews, the way he leans forward eagerly, widens his eyes, punches out every word with practiced vivacity.

We've all heard the explanations for why Michael is at ease only when he is with children. His reasons make a kind of psychological sense. Children are open and unpredictable. Children are creative and playful. Children are true innocents. Children give joy and want joy in return. Children ask nothing of you but love and protection. You can capture your lost childhood in the company of children.

Michael never admits that he is angry as well as lonely and sad. And yet, what better reproach to all grown-ups—family, siblings, fans—than to have nothing to do with them except as businesspeople you can hire and fire. Or as wives you can marry and divorce. Or as surrogate mothers you can pay and dismiss.

Sometimes when I think back on that infamous photograph of Michael Jackson holding his baby over the balcony of a hotel, I see it as a child star's act of vengeance. Holding a baby over a balcony is furious, infantile acting-out—doing something outrageous when people are interfering with you. "You follow me, you hound me, you won't leave me alone, you want to see me, you want to see my baby, fine. Here's my baby. If I drop him, if he falls, it's all your fault."

We talk about how we think, believe, suspect Michael Jackson treats children. We don't talk about how *we* treat child stars. Child stars are abused by the culture. And what's more treacherous than when the rewards of child stardom issue from the abuse? Child stars are performers above all else. Whatever their triumphs, they are going to make sure we see every one of their scars. That's the final price of admission.

Alone of All His Race,
Alone of All Her Sex

In the past two decades we've watched Michael Jackson morph from a slender brown-skinned man to a slightly anorexic white-skinned . . . what? Look at the face and you might see a transsexual, while the wardrobe suggests a gothic dandy. Often he wears a military uniform or a suit. Always an armband, almost always a medallion. Brocade shirts and ties, often in pastel colors. But it's the face. Is it black or white, male or female? There is no realism here, only mythology. The face is a ceremonial mask, gorgonlike. It is affixed; it was achieved through surgery.

Never have so many people around the world—but especially in the United States—had plastic surgery of some kind. *The Swan, Extreme Makeover, Dr. Beverly Hills 90210*—television had to catch up with real life to put on these docudramas of extreme need

79

and desire. But most people want an improved version of themselves, or at least something they could call a beautiful relation. Michael's face is in another zone altogether. It has nothing in common with him anymore. We look. We shiver. We want to turn away. He was not supposed to expose this kind of need. What is it: Self-hatred? Fear and loathing of human beings? A passion to escape the conditions of life and human exchange so fierce that he is willing to be reborn through science? The desire for a kind of perfection most of us cannot see and that he will not share with us? A will to change reality that is a postmodern version of hubris?

Michael's gender crossover began with the hair and makeup of the mid- and late eighties, when his complexion was still a distinct shade of brown. It then lightened and became whitish. By the early nineties his face was chalk-white, a fact that registered with the same shock a sex-change operation might provoke. He was even wearing eyeliner and lipstick and sporting beauty-shop hairdos. At first, people talked more openly about the whitening than about the femme-ing. Probably because a skin change was something that blacks, whites and others—gays, straights, bis and trannies—could righteously agree on. The mantra was: "Self-hatred is awful, shameful, pathetic."

Personally, I reached a point where I did not wish to discuss the matter or share the sadness with one

more sympathetically pained white person. I was con-
founded. Michael's state made all the old-style metaphors of black self-hatred passé. What's the point of
calling someone an Oreo (black on the outside, white
on the inside) when he isn't even trying to be black on
the outside? When a charge like "You must think you're
white" becomes literal instead of behavioral, what is
one to do? The cost of racial self-loathing has long
been established. For many people, the gender change
was more complicated. Not that they were necessarily
more comfortable about homosexuals, transvestites
or transsexuals than with the sight of a black man
turning white. But if they were at all liberal, if they
were pop culture lovers, they were less comfortable
about sounding judgmental.

At the time, the artist Keith Haring was refresh-
ingly nonjudgmental: A 1987 journal entry reads, "I
talk about my respect for Michael's attempts to take
creation in his own hands and invent a non-black,
non-white, non-male, non-female creature by utilizing
plastic surgery and modern technology. He's totally
Walt-Disneyed out! An interesting phenomenon at the
least. A little scary, maybe, but nonetheless remarkable,
and I think somehow a healthier example than Rambo
or Ronald Reagan. He's denied the finality of God's
creation and taken it into his own hands, while all the
time parading around in front of American pop culture. I think it would be much cooler if he would go all

81

the way and get his ears pointed or add a tail or something, but give him time!"[1] Michael, it turned out, had
some surprises up his sleeve.

By the early nineties everything was being acted
out and hidden—flaunted and denied at the same
time. Yes, he said in interviews, he'd had plastic surgery. But only a few operations, not the reported fifty.
No, he finally told Oprah Winfrey in 1993, he had not
had his skin lightened, he was suffering from vitiligo
and had to wear makeup to even out the tones. It was
very painful for him. Above and beyond all that, his
life was about healing race divisions. But he couldn't
heal the truth-versus-damage-control split that everyone watching him sensed. Plenty of people felt the
vitiligo story was a lie. And if it was true, some said,
why not handle it more effectively? Make a statement
before you're pushed to make a confession, have a press
conference to announce that you have a disease for
which there is no real cure. Say it is difficult to bear,
painful to talk about. Ask for people's understanding
and love—not just for you, but also for the millions of
sufferers whose names they do not know.

Some two hundred years ago, scientists were quick to
explain what it meant when a black person turned
white. But first they had to explain why people were
black, brown, red and yellow to begin with. All human

beings had descended from one original man and woman, went the most popular theory. Therefore the environment—climate, diet, general way of life—was responsible for variations in looks, behavior, intelligence, civilization. In 1787 an American scientist named Samuel Stanhope Smith published accounts of how some of the Irish and Germans who had immigrated to the United States and been thrown into the same "savage state" as native-born Indians were growing darker. A welcome contrast was the occasional Indian who grew noticeably lighter and more keen-featured after enrolling in college.

Increasingly, African-Americans became the object of these observations, not just in medical journals, but in the popular press. Two white women who had married black men grew darker, reported Dr. Benjamin Rush, who believed that the Negro's color was the result of leprosy, and perhaps infectious. But in most observed cases, the process was reversed. Gradually, by degrees, of course. One Negro began to go white around his abdomen; the color spread and after seven years (the classic biblical time of feast or famine) he was mostly white. Another Negro began to achieve whiteness as a teenager: first there were white spots, then the spots increased in number and finally only a few brown specks remained.[2]

"Albinos" can be found in every ethnic group, though. A seventeenth-century historian, Balthazar

Tellez, coined the term when he saw tribes with very pale members along the coast of West Africa. In 1869 a doctor named Joseph Jones linked vitiligo to albinism. Albinism could be a slave's road to freedom, according to Dr. Jones. One black slave whose skin paled (dark spots, of course, remained) and whose hair turned blond and silky found himself a free man when the whites he lived among paid to release him from bondage.

For years Michael broke race rules and made us love it. First he made a black boy as winningly universal as Tom Sawyer or Huck Finn. Then he made himself into an enchanting teen idol. His adult persona was even more brilliant, if troubling. He was a mélange of genres and periods: pieces of Fred Astaire and Sammy Davis Jr.; a touch of Diana Ross; soul, funk, disco and rock. But let's look back at the customs of the race world he grew up in.

What links every term invented for or by people of African descent about people of African descent is an obsession with skin color, hair texture, features (the size of the nose and lips especially) and body type. Status, too, of course, and behavior. But it all starts with looks. Negars, Ethiopes, Senegambians, Negroes, colored people, black people, people of color, Aframericans, African-Americans; nigger, nigga, coon, boot;

splib. Mulatto, quadroon, octoroon, piece of yellow, high yellow, high brown, seal brown, marigny (fair to pale with light hair and sub-Saharan features) or black as the ace of spades.

Traditionally, a dark-skinned woman with nappy hair was not a great catch for either a light-skinned man or a dark-skinned man with social ambitions. But the kind of features described as keen or chiseled could ennoble a dark complexion, female or male, and yield a look admiringly described as Ethiopian. Joseph Jackson, Michael's father, was medium to light brown with green eyes, great assets by certain Negro standards. His other features would have been found less impressive: bushy eyebrows, bulky face, broad nose, full lips. Katherine Scruggs Jackson was dark café au lait, almost the same color as the young Diana Ross. But Katherine had high cheekbones (Indian blood, surely) and soft almond eyes. Her lips were not thick. She must have been told often what a sweet smile she had.

The Jackson boys got their father's nose. Their skin was darker than Katherine's—which was fine. They were boys. Rebbie and La Toya were lighter than Joseph and had pert noses, small mouths and the bright, obliging smiles of midwestern girls at the state fair. Baby Janet got her mother's skin and a pug nose, which she considered a drawback once she began to have teen-queen aspirations. The face of Michael Jackson that we see today has nothing to do with his genetic inheritance from Joseph and Katherine, being wholly a product of surgery, cosmetology and fashion. Michael doesn't look like anything we can correlate with experience. That's why people keep saying things like "He's absolutely crazy. I believe he could do anything," or "He may be guilty of nothing more than being the strangest person on the planet," or "All right, so he's a perv. But does he even have a penis?" When we say "It's so sad, it's tragic," we're talking about the genius performer. We're also talking about the mystery of why someone would voluntarily pass over into the world of solitary freakdom.

Michael had his first nose job in 1979, and a second, improved one a year later. He was twenty-one. When his brothers had been in the mood to tease him, they had called him "Big Nose" and "Liver Lips." Sotto voce, though, black people have been known to joke that when you look at his brothers today, you understand why Michael chose surgical intervention, even though he went much too far. "Self-hatred" is a term flung about with glib authority, but here it's hard to avoid. It seems to have started early at 2300 Jackson Street.

Stars treat cosmetic surgery as their prerogative. For some it's a necessity, and you know why when you see their relatives being interviewed for some E! Entertainment Television biography. These relatives aren't usually ugly, just ordinary looking. The bad luck of the biological draw? Sometimes. A matter of not having enough money to spend on top-of-the-line haircuts, makeup and clothes? Often. But it's rhinoplasty, cheek implants, Botox-firm foreheads and collagen-stuffed lips that make the real difference. Still, most stars use surgery to maintain a high-gloss version of a face we recognize. Michael Jackson presents an unrecognizable, alien face to the world. Why?

He has said over and over in interviews that he is obsessed with perfection. He will rehearse hour after hour, working till he gets a move or routine exactly right. Yet, his appearance is always in perilous flux. Time and again in his videos we see Michael undergoing monstrous transformations: from sweet young man to ghoul (*Thriller*); from natty pop star to black cat (*Billie Jean*); from dancing white-robed shaman to hooligan smashing windows, then seizing and stroking his penis (*Black or White*); from raging hooligan to Buddha (*Scream*). He loves genres that emphasize mutable identities, carefree cartoons and horror tales. And it's mutability that makes his dancing so special. That ability to smoothly turn a James Brown funky chicken into Josephine Baker's knock-kneed Charleston. The quick jumps. The pelvic thrusts in profile (one knee held up) that give way to sleek jazz runs. He has the ability to be liquid *and* percussive all at once, to create an aura of suspense and improvisation.

When he became a solo artist, Michael Jackson started inventing not only personae but fashion as well. You couldn't pin him down to one style. On the cover of the 1979 album *Off the Wall* he wears a tux with a white dress shirt and black bow tie. He stands against a brick wall (*no more urban blight for me!*), legs apart in vaudeville's classic "Look out world, here I come" stance. His thumbs are in his pockets, his fingers extended; he hitches his pant legs up ever so slightly. We follow the line of the straight-cut black pants down to white socks and patent-leather loafers. The right toe turns in a fraction, making the right pant leg hang at a slight angle. The white socks glow as brightly as Dorothy's ruby slippers.

"Style is a mode of confrontation."[3] Michael the dandy, the fashionista, who once dreamed of having Jackie Wilson's patent leather shoes, made dippy white socks just as cool—and just as hot. Offstage he was still finding his way. Over the next few years, fanciful print shirts and quality sports jackets in small checks gave way to boatneck pullovers; white button-down shirts with rolled-up sleeves and easy white slacks; jeans and a satin motorcycle jacket.

On the brothers' 1984 "Victory" tour reunion, Michael plays with his tux, rolling the jacket sleeves above his elbows and unfastening one of his shirt cuffs. It's the Gypsy Rose Lee effect. A single wrist, uncuffed and bared: let it be the merest hint of nakedness. Flash back to 1979's video of "Rock With You": Michael wears a soft, clinging jumpsuit in glittery black and silver stripes. It moves with his body. He undulates but does nothing flashy. He looks delicately nubile. He is in transit.

He has arrived in *Thriller*. The album background is gray-black. Michael lounges front and center in a white suit with easy folds. The belt is lizard, the shirt casual. It unzips to the middle of Michael's smooth chest. He sports an animal print pocket square. Open the album jacket and, in another picture, you will see that detail picked up by the baby tiger hanging over Michael's raised knee. The camera lingers on the veins in Michael's hands and neck, the line of the (still very pretty) nose, the full brown eyes. The light casts a glow on parts of his caramel brown skin and on the back curls of his hair. Perhaps the two curls dangling over his forehead are a bit much. Overdone curls always signal anxiety. But that's a quibble. The eyebrows have been plucked and penciled—tastefully, of course. It's 1982 and this is pop music's version of the Hollywood studio portrait and the fashion layout.

The art of Michael's face—features, makeup, hair—grew ever more extreme in the years after *Thriller*. So did the wardrobe, an equally audacious act of self-authorship. Every fan wanted the red leather jacket with tiny pleats that he wore in the title video where he turns into a werewolf. (Call it a red alert.)

Every fan wanted the red leather jacket of *Beat It*, where he rushes into the street to stop a rumble between rival gangs. (A red badge of courage and chic.) In the "Billie Jean" video he danced alone in a black leather suit with a white shirt and spats; his feet moved lightly across translucent squares that turned to gold dust then disappeared.

Oiled and gelled hair now brushed his shoulders. Sometimes it was pressed flat into a hairline that curved around his skull like a bathing beauty's swim cap. A few long curls draped the forehead. Plenty of black men were going for the luxuriant Jheri-curl treatment then. Prince and El DeBarge had straighter hair than Michael, so they went for heads of glossy Latin curls. Plenty of white men still had shoulder-length hair and high-maintenance cuts (Hall and Oates were prime examples). But Michael's hair had a beauty-shop look. The curls and waves, the way the hair was pulled back at his ears. Hairstyles always imply certain gestures. Michael's implied that he could flick it behind his ears the way young white girls do. And he did so occasionally at awards ceremonies.

In photographs of him with Diana Ross from this period, they look uncannily alike. They have the same nose (straight, gently rounded at the nostrils); similar mouths (his is wider, her upper lip is fuller); similar dark eyes and firmly but lightly drawn eyebrows. She gazes grandly in the camera; he gazes quietly. She wears

the mask of star glamour (Joan Crawford at a pre-
miere), he the mask of mournful genius (Chaplin
without his mustache). But on the cover of *Ebony* magazine, hand in hand at a gala, they turn their heads
toward the camera at the same angle, and their flash-
bulb smiles ("Here, bask in my glow for a moment")
are identical.

Of course there was competition. Michael was the
new young deity in town—the younger, fresher object
of aesthetic and sexual desire. Their twinned, sometimes merging identities tantalized. Urban sexual
myths sprang up. Michael wrote a song for Diana, supposedly about his pet snake. When she curled her
breathy languid voice around the words "I want muscles," one could imagine the desire as Michael's. When
she sang "I'm Coming Out," one could dream that she
spoke for Michael.

Those were glorious times. The late 1980s and the
1990s became his angst-ridden "Am I man enough?"
period. The years of challenges to homeboys who
threatened ("Bad" and "Dangerous"); to white lawyers
and businessmen who tried to control him ("2 Bad,"
"Invincible"); and to black men whose cultural and
commercial power rivaled his (in *Jam* he outshoots
and outdances Michael Jordan). The women were
meaner than Billie Jean, and greedier; there was
groupie and sexual predator "Dirty Diana" and a girl-
friend named Susie who left blood on the dance floor

with a phallic knife that went "seven inches in." ("You're dirty, you're nasty," he chanted in one song—to himself or to the woman?) The luscious model Naomi Campbell danced seductively for him in one video, and for her trouble got told (with an emphatic flamenco stance), "Whatever we do, keep it in the closet."

Hip-hop was starting to close in on Michael Jackson's territory. He was fighting to maintain his place in the pop myth hierarchy. He had a rare victory with his 1988 video *Smooth Criminal* because he staged the fight on his own stylistic terms. It is one of his innocence-tracked-by-evil songs. A criminal enters an apartment and attacks a little girl; she flees to the bedroom, leaving bloodstains on the carpet. All to the refrain, chanted and whispered, "Annie, are you okay, Annie, are you okay, are you okay, Annie?" It is also a fairy-tale thriller in which Michael the good merges with Michael the killer.

As it opens, horns sound a theme of martial triumph and strings soar. Three children (two boys—one white, one black—and a white girl with blonde pigtails) perch on a fence across from a dark building. With them we watch Michael come down an alley in a cream suit with matching hat and spats. He pauses in front of the building's closed door, then pushes it open. There's a rush of white light. He touches his hat with resolve, as cowboys do when they're about to face down a saloon of enemies.

It's a gambling dive that could also be an opium den (we see an Asian woman in a plumed sequined headband) and it's an homage to James Cagney's fabulous song-and-dance number "Shanghai Lil" in the 1933 musical *Footlight Parade.* Cagney plays a producer who stars in his own "prologue"—it might as well be a music video—as a sailor seeking his lady in a cheap waterfront bar.

In Michael's bar, mostly black and Latin men wear thirties and forties gangster gear: cuffed pants, colored shirts, suspenders and hats. The women (mostly black, Latin and Asian) have the spangled and ruffled saloon mistress look of Marlene Dietrich in *Destry Rides Again.*

A coin flips from Michael's hand to the jukebox. A downbeat and a body spasm launch the number. It plays synchronized limbs against fragmented body parts. True to its multigenre setting, *Smooth Criminal* is a compendium of movie fight scenes. Michael slides and struts. His arms cut through the air; his chin juts out and back. He does a few tango steps with one woman, climbs the stairs and does a few grinds at the top with another. The men are rough criminals and— elegantly—Michael out-roughs them. He breaks the pool cue of one and blows dust in his face. "C'mon, c'mon," another threatens. Michael slinks toward him with mockingly pointed toes ("You think I'm not a real man?") and delivers an elbow to his solar plexus. A third man approaches from behind brandishing a shiny dagger; without turning around, Michael snatches a gun from his breast pocket and fires. The camera shifts to the window, where the little girl with pigtails watches. Annie, are you okay?

Suddenly the crowd grows more frenzied—heads thrust forward and back, their knees spread open. Bullets shatter a window; silence; a black cat moves down the piano keys. Michael starts to moan; the moan is taken up as the men and women form a circle around him. He bends and nods in a trance; they chant "Annie, are you okay?" This could be a voodoo ritual.

But the frenzy breaks up into a svelte nightclub number for Michael and four men. At one magical point, they stand up straight and tilt in unison toward the floor. A bit of soft shoe, then the women join in to primp, posture, isolate and flaunt body parts (shoulders, hips, calves) in Bob Fosse style. "That's cool, huh? I taught him everything he knows," says the little black boy who also watches through a window. Then *he* cuts some smooth criminal hip-hop moves in his blue jeans and overcoat.

The video ends with the violence Michael so loves. The shadow of gunmen outside the windows, the blast of machine-guns, and Michael slips out. The Asian woman leans against the door, spent. The miracle has passed.

Offscreen, there is now a toyland quality to Michael's wardrobe. Military jackets replete with gold braid. Military jackets in bright beaded fabrics with gold; deep blue with turquoise collar and gold epaulettes; ribbons across his chest. Always, they nip the waist. "Mother, sister, lover" Diana is replaced by mother, counselor and best friend Elizabeth Taylor. When he accompanies her to the American Music Awards in 1986, he wears the military look that a European monarch who leads a cavalry might: belted-below-the-waist jacket, jodhpurs and knee-high riding boots. His eyebrows are darkened and arch more heavily than before: see Elizabeth Taylor in *Butterfield 8* and *Cleopatra*. See that smolderingly gorgeous 1950s studio portrait of Taylor with bare shoulders and white mink stole.

The lipstick grows brighter. The features look even more chiseled. All this atop black leather gear for 1987's *Bad* album cover. The ebony sheen of the jacket matches the ebony sheen of the hair. Soft curls are countered by silver studs and zippers. The arms are akimbo in the pose of the street tough; one hand rests just below the studded belt buckle, the other just above. A flash of white collar against the whitening skin of the neck and face, then the stark white of the album cover. "Bad" is scrawled in graffiti red; "Michael

Jackson" is black block letters. Ebony and ivory. Think of one of Jean Paul Gaultier's rampaging leather-boy outfits. Think of Queen's Freddie Mercury, bestriding the rock world like a camp colossus.

When we say "cross-dressing" we think of one-to-one exchange. Female to male. Male to female. Michael looked more like a gender work in progress. Or a gender game in which the rules were always changing. The face looked as though it had found safe passage from male to female. But the clothes were a whimsical fantasy parade. The uniforms: storybook military. The black pants and turtleneck: fashion magazine beatnik. (He could have done the beatniks-in-Paris scene with—or as—Audrey Hepburn in *Funny Face*.) The black pants and white shirts: song-and-dance Gene Kelly, Judy Garland. The androgynous American sportswear look of Gap ads also had its place.

The lean body is androgynous too. But the big hands look manly. They're Fred Astaire hands. Those hands were Astaire's manliest attribute. I don't mean to suggest he was womanly. Astaire was neither/nor, as is Michael Jackson. Both men channeled eros into the dance, and the dance reveals an emotional agenda that is never revealed elsewhere. "You're an angry dancer," Astaire told him. "I used to do that with my cane." Michael does it with canes, corkscrew kicks and pelvic thrusts. His long fingers (four of the tips often bandaged) are often lunging for his penis.

It's a kind of stripper's taunt. I'll preen, I'll point, I'll fondle my private parts. Look, I'll open my shirt—here's my bare chest—but I ain't taking nothing off. Michael plays up, down and around masculine sexuality. Michael Jackson, the performer, has never offered portraits of black or white masculinity that are at all realistic or, better, conventional.[4]

In *Invisible Man*, Ralph Ellison wrote that the challenge for a black artist "was not actually one of creating the uncreated conscience of his race, but of creating the uncreated features of his face." Maybe "unacknowledged" is a better word than "uncreated," but Michael Jackson has met the challenge. Is his new face really as alien as we all want to believe? How many black, brown, yellow and red people haven't somewhere, at some time, wanted to look white? And how many white people haven't looked in the mirror and wanted to look like anything but what they saw there? America is obsessed with nips, tucks, Botox and rhinoplasty: never have so many people worked so hard to create new faces for themselves. "We create the race by creating ourselves," wrote Ellison.

Race and gender passers need to reimagine themselves. To present that vision as authentic they must be great performers. In the old days passing was supposed to be a perfect imitation of life, flawlessly realistic. If anything about the passer raised doubts (Is that how a white person really talks? Is that how a man really walks?), the performance had failed. Michael Jackson has changed all that. He imitates no kind of life known to us. He passes in plain sight. Each appearance through the years has been a rehearsal, a restaging. Our doubts are never soothed, our questions never answered. Passers are supposed to hide their past, shed their racial or sexual history. Michael's past is everywhere. It exists in thousands of photographs and film images. He makes no attempt to hide it.

"The Negro . . . is primarily an artist . . . His *métier* is expression rather than action. He is, so to speak, the lady among the races."[5] When the white sociologist Robert E. Park said this in 1918, black intellectuals responded with understandable outrage. Nor did black male musical artists—bluesmen, jazzmen—have any use for this feminized vision of themselves. But Michael has made use of it. He took it up and bound it to a black gay aesthetic that has been pushed to the margins of black culture: drag balls, voguing, club life and biracial and gender-bending eros. When Michael and his sister La Toya are photographed side by side, it's as if ghostly twins have just floated out of a gothic mansion. They could be Roderick and Madeline, the tormented siblings in Edgar Allan Poe's "The Fall of the House of Usher." Janet blends right in when the three of them appear together, as they did in court early on in Michael's trial, swathed in flowing white garments, eyes hidden by white-framed dark glasses. The sisters' hair cascaded below their shoulders. Michael's fell softly to his shoulders, then curled upward (the 1960s Jackie Kennedy flip). Their resemblance was uncanny. A war of gender worlds had been going on in the Jackson family for decades, and Michael had a long time ago chosen to join the women.

Michael's first black female role model was his mother, Katherine: Katherine the good; Katherine the loving; Katherine who believed in art and the imagination. Then came Diana Ross—"mother, sister, lover"—who taught him about style, manners, attitude, how to carry himself as he moved beyond the confines of the Motown family. When he became a son of Hollywood, he found a mother in Elizabeth Taylor; when he decided to write a book, he found a female icon in his editor, Jacqueline Onassis. The physical trajectory is clear: from the black supermodel Diana Ross, to palely exotic Liz Taylor, to the ethereal Jackie O.

And consider the metaphoric link between Michael and aging female stars, who cope with the passage of time by retreating to a protective haven that excludes most other adults. There they devote themselves to

female? 99

loving creatures who need protection, usually dogs: Brigitte Bardot, Doris Day, Kim Novak. Do we know that Michael doesn't feel exactly this way toward his children and young boys in general? Well-treated dogs give unconditional love. So do well-treated children. And if you are a man who wants to love and who fears sex, you are better off with children most like yourself: boys. And if you are a man trapped in the traumas of your childhood, you are going to be drawn to—moved by—your own kind: young boys who have suffered as you did.

Michael Jackson has been a sexual impersonator since age five. As a child, he played adolescents and men. Once he became a man, he played up, down and around masculine sexuality. The real erotic power was always in the rhythms of his voice and body. He was more a god of dance and song than a man intimating the danger and pleasure of real sex. And the hottest songs are usually about dancing: "Don't Stop Till You Get Enough," "Off the Wall," "Rock with You," "Blood on the Dance Floor." It's trance music.

Michael has been singing (and speaking) in a breathy falsetto all of his adult life. The counterpoint was his compulsive crotch grabbing, which began in the 1980s, even as his face started looking more feminine and rumors about his sexual proclivities spread. On one level the videos were like manhood contests. *The Way You Make Me Feel* was a neighborhood romance with the feel of a *Playboy* magazine spread: boys looking at hot models. He was seducing a pretty young woman while all the boys looked on admiringly. In *Bad*, one of his street gang videos, he was fighting off tough guys and looking prettier too. They were rough-hewn and dark; he was slim and light, with what was supposed to look like good hair—again, by certain Negro standards.

The phallus-worship section of 1991's *Black or White* was cut from some versions after intense viewer protests. It is a fiercely jarring coda to a vision of folkloric global amity. Wearing black (pants) and white (shirt), Michael dances with different peoples of the world. Each wears native dress, and, for a few measures, his fluent body adapts to each indigenous dance. He stands atop the Statue of Liberty and atop a Russian onion dome. He presides over a technological ethnic meltdown, as men and women from various groups morph into one another, trading faces and features. Then we're in the studio where the video has been shot. "That was great," the (white) director, John Landis, tells the young woman whose light-brown skin and curly hair were last on the screen.

And then comes the dark night of Michael's racial

and sexual soul. The video goes from bright clean color to black and white. We are in an alley. A black panther is on the prowl and he turns into Michael Jackson now in a black shirt, dancing as if possessed. "Hitler lives" is scrawled on a car window; "KKK Rules" on the glass panes of a door. (This graffiti was added to the video after shocked viewers protested Michael's frenzied rage.) Michael utters long cries; he shatters the offending glass with a garbage can and the car's steering wheel. And he dances—a violent tap dance without real tap sounds. Which makes it oddly ominous—we see and feel the percussion but we don't hear it. It creates a strange tension. Partly because it's sinuous and elegant—the way soft-shoe tap is. And very much because every few beats he strokes, snatches at, caresses his . . . phallus. The inevitable climax is averted (or completed) when Michael turns into a big panther, haunches gleaming as he moves into the night.

In retrospect, the crotch clutch seems at once desperate and abstract. It is as if he were telling us, "Fine, you need to know I'm a man, a black man? Here's my dick: I'll thrust my dick at you! Isn't that what a black man's supposed to do? But I'm Michael Jackson, so just look but you can't touch." It wasn't real, it was symbolic. Not a penis but a phallus.

We sometimes underestimate how many styles of black masculinity there are. Call it the many modes of virility. Player, brute, sweet man, pretty boy, hustler, to name a few. We sometimes forget how much of the feminine and the homoerotic can be found here. The dandy, the gent and the tough merge with the church choir leader and the queen: think of Little Richard.

Michael has never cited Little Richard as an influence. True, Richard Penniman hit his stride before James Brown and Jackie Wilson, the honored fathers of Michael's musical genealogy, hit theirs. Still, it's odd, especially since James Brown has acknowledged Little Richard as an influence. When artists cite their influences, they always leave certain important figures out. The legacy is unsettling—to the artists' self-image or to public expectations. But surely Little Richard, rock and roll's first out-and-out queer man, the king and queen of rock and roll—with his face powder, eyebrow pencil and lipstick; his beauty shop, not barbershop hair; and his gospel diva cries—deserves to be honored too. "You're gonna make me scream like a white lady," he was known to shout during performances, in a style that was outrageously comic. It's worth remembering that where Little Richard went, few black men followed. (There was quite a gap between Liberace and Freddie Mercury too.) Mass pop music culture did not have a vast space for queer performers—certainly not for performers with a flagrantly femme style. Many stayed in the gospel church. A few, like Sylvester, found a space in the club and disco culture of the 1970s. I am not saying that Michael Jackson is gay. I am saying that he draws on gay culture—its signs and codes—but pretends that he doesn't and that we shouldn't notice.

In 1995, Michael Jackson gave a strangely spectacular performance at the MTV Awards. It brought masculinity and femininity together in just proportions. It was a rare occasion.

Scene one, the Nightclub Diva: Blue light shows the outline of an absolutely still body. It's in shadow, so you linger on its shape: the wide shoulders, long legs and arms; the outsized hands. Then a spotlight comes on. Then another and another. Michael is wearing black pants, a black jacket and a white shirt. His hair is a refined, nineties version of a sixties bubble. When the music starts (a pounding beat), he tears the jacket off (dandy into rocker) and throws himself into a taut medley of "The Way You Make Me Feel," "Billie Jean," "Beat It," and the aggressive bridge from "Black or White." Slash, the rock guitarist, in heavy metal leather, jewelry and top hat, runs on. This incites Michael to a frenzy as if possessed; he tears around the stage, uttering pitched cries, doing African squats and falling on his knees as smoke engulfs them both.

Scene two, the Old-School Vaudeville Trouper: Empty stage. Michael is behind a scrim. When it rises, he wears a beaded sweater jacket (the kind Judy Garland wore, but with more flash around the neck). Now he pulls out some of his celebrated moves. The leg that kicks or twists (but there are fewer twists now). The

Moonwalk (but just for a few measures). The fast turns (but not as many and slower than before). In aging diva style, he compensates with a few new tricks, some stylish hip-hop moves.

Scene three, the Hollywood Musical Entertainer: Michael wears a white shirt, a thin black tie and a fedora. He's flanked by a half dozen or so men dressed in suits, each wearing one red glove. The beat is Afro-Cuban, the songs are "Smooth Criminal" and "Dangerous." Nightclub jazz infused with Dietrich and Ross, Astaire and Sammy Davis.

The theater of gender has scripts galore, so many to choose from. But, as the great actor John Gielgud used to say, "style is knowing what play you're in." Rarely does Michael Jackson seem to know this anymore.

The Trial

The Charges

> **Count 1:** Conspiracy to commit child abduction, false imprisonment and extortion.
>
> **Count 2:** Lewd act on a child under fourteen.
>
> **Count 3:** Lewd act on a child under fourteen.
>
> **Count 4:** Lewd act on a child under fourteen.
>
> **Count 5:** Lewd act on a child under fourteen.
>
> **Count 6:** Attempted lewd act on a child under fourteen.
>
> **Count 7:** Administering alcohol to enable child molestation.
>
> **Count 8:** Administering alcohol to enable child molestation.
>
> **Count 9:** Administering alcohol to enable child molestation.
>
> **Count 10:** Administering alcohol to enable child molestation.

The Principal Characters

Prosecuting attorney THOMAS SNEDDON JR.: Santa
Barbara district attorney Thomas Sneddon is tall and
broad-shouldered with a rough, ruddy complexion
and a moustache that all but bristles. He is nearly bald,
but in the land of hair dye and hair plugs he makes no
effort to conceal it. He wears severe rimless glasses and
speaks in a flat, gruff voice. Like Joseph Jackson, he is
the father of nine children. For years, lawyer colleagues
have called him "Mad Dog." He pursued the 1993 case
against Michael Jackson obsessively, it is said, and was
furious and humiliated when an out-of-court settlement thwarted his chance to send the superstar to
prison. Feature writers like to invoke Victor Hugo's
Inspector Javert. But Sneddon is more like the stolid,
truculent policeman in a Ross Macdonald novel. Or
one by Jim Thompson, if you want to play up the
obsessive, "Mad Dog Inside Me" angle.

The one thing he shares with Michael Jackson is an
unsavory history of lawsuits. In 2003, Sneddon and his
office faced eleven. The best-known case involved
Efren Cruz, a man accused of robbery who served
eleven years in prison before an appeals court ordered
his release on the grounds that Sneddon's office had
withheld evidence—a full confession by two other
men—that proved his innocence.

On November 19, 2003, the day after the spectacular police raid of Jackson's estate, Thomas Sneddon gives a press conference. Sheriff Jim Anderson, who led the seventy police officers plus a team of search dogs through Neverland, is also present. But this is Sneddon's show. The day before, Jackson's lawyer, Mark Geragos (with his big, dark mustache, a head of thinning hair and big movie-star sunglasses), had issued a warning: "We will land on you like a ton of bricks," he thundered into a gaggle of microphones. "We will land on you like a hammer. If you do anything to besmirch this man's reputation, anything to intrude on his privacy in any way that's actionable, we will unleash a legal torrent like you've never seen."

It is his version of "Bring it on." Now Sneddon must strike back, and he begins by showing the press, the public and the world that he is not unduly obsessed with Michael Jackson; he is not brooding over a ten-year-old defeat. The potential for something along the lines of Nixon's feverish "I am not a crook" speech is there. But Sneddon handles himself well. His department biography notes that after years of bearing the "Mad Dog" moniker, the DA is now "affectionately known as 'Snuffy.' " Both personae are on display at this press conference and together they work the room. First, Mad Dog reminds the reporters of just how little they know about the law or sex crimes. "Commonly, in these kinds of cases—let me clarify something because some of you are not lawyers, and I don't want you to get it wrong . . . Just so we all understand, we're talking about a violation of 288(a), child molesting, not oral copulation of an adult—or of children. Okay, so I want to clarify that, so that you understand that." He softens the press up momentarily—"I couldn't resist the temptation to watch a little bit of some of this coverage last night on TV"—then he raps their knuckles: a lot of them, he says, were "apologists for Mr. Jackson." The "them" refers to reporters who have quoted a statement by Jackson to the effect that his album was released the same day as the raid and that "these characters always seem to surface with dreadful allegations just as another project, an album, a video, is being released."

Sneddon explains that his office couldn't execute the warrant before because fifty thousand people came to the area for Halloween. He is impassive when he begins to play for laughs. He says the warrant's timing had "nothing to do with Jackson's album," then, with a "you know kids and their shenanigans" grin, adds, "or whatever else he's doing in his life." Mad Dog makes clear that as far as he's concerned Michael Jackson is a criminal who needs to get his overdressed butt to the sheriff's office as fast as his private plane will allow. He refuses to answer specific questions about the case. He gets somewhat churlish when Jackson seems to be getting too much of the reporters' attention. When Sneddon is asked if the star is still in Las Vegas, his voice rises just slightly: "I don't know. I mean, we really have a life other than Michael Jackson, and we've been trying to work on our own investigation, as you well know, because I saw it on TV before I came down here." Could he talk about his satisfaction at finally bringing Jackson to justice? He won't take the bait. "When that case went to bed, ten years ago, it was out of my mind. . . .

"You folks and people keep calling every time he does a bizarre thing to ask me my comment about it. But I have—I really do have—a lot of things going on, as do the sheriff, former sheriff, and people in my office. We really have a very busy office. I haven't given it a passing thought."

Then Snuffy—Sneddon's alter ego—appears. Snuffy's only feelings are for the victim and his family. He feels bad for them, he says; he feels bad that there is "another victim out there." But throughout the trial, Mad Dog will undercut Snuffy. Courtroom reporters will write about how Sneddon rolls his eyes and grimaces whenever a prosecution witness fails to produce what he wants. Lawyers begin to criticize him, even patronize him, for putting undue emphasis on the shaky conspiracy charges. Jackson's conspiring to whisk the victim and his family away in a hot air balloon? Locking them up at Neverland when the mother was free to go shopping, see the dentist and go to a nearby spa for a bikini wax? Not the strongest of cases.

If Sneddon is smart, he will announce he is dropping the conspiracy charges and force the jury to focus entirely on the sexual molestation counts. But he isn't the kind of man who will admit he made a tactical mistake, even if doing so might be to his advantage. Sneddon's press conference after the verdict will make this clear. He will speak slowly, with heavy pauses, like a man trying to get his breath back. His statement? His team did their job. You win some, you lose some. Bad breaks, setbacks.

MICHAEL JOSEPH JACKSON: Those convinced of Jackson's guilt see him as a pop Count Dracula who invites families into his castle, then lures the children away to frolic, feast and develop a taste for the forbidden. Once they fall under his spell, he has his way with them. (Even the wine he was said to call "Jesus juice" conjures up the image of innocent blood defiled.) Those convinced of his innocence see a man who gives of his talent and his love unceasingly; a charitable man who works to end war, help children and set an example of universal understanding; an innocent man who saves lives and brings joy to troubled souls around the world. His oddness is his wound. It might well cause his martyrdom.

On November 23, Michael Jackson flies to Santa Barbara from Las Vegas, where he has been filming a video for a now-canceled television special. He is filmed entering the sheriff's office in a black suit, a white shirt with a narrow stand-up collar, sunglasses and handcuffs. This is known as the perp walk. Jackson is booked, fingerprinted and photographed. He posts a three-million-dollar bail and leaves the building. He gives fans and photographers his familiar "victory" peace sign, then climbs back into his car and is driven away uncuffed but flanked by police officers on motorcycles.

He leaves behind a mug shot that quickly becomes the shot seen round the world. Till the trial ends it appears on Web sites and television shows, in newspapers and magazines. He looks like a haggard drag queen stunned by the daylight. Has someone yanked his Joan Crawford eyebrows into that spooky arch and pinned them there? Is the nose even real? The coral lipstick looks harsh and cheap against the pale skin: police lighting brings out the worst undertones in anyone's makeup and complexion.

Michael Jackson makes his first court appearance on January 16, 2004. It is his attempt to put a star stamp on the proceedings, and it is deemed a failure. The late arrival? Self-indulgence or disconnect. The Fruit of Islam bodyguards, recommended by brother Jermaine? A quick, unconvincing "I am a proud black man scorned and 'bused by white people" fix. (It doesn't help that Jermaine has followed Clarence Thomas's rhetorical lead and called the prosecution "a lynching.") Jumping on top of his SUV when he leaves court and acquitting himself of a few dance moves for his fans? Doesn't he realize he's out of shape—that his moves don't cut it anymore? Is he mad? Does he know how serious this is?

Here's an ugly fact: the sexual abuse of children largely goes underreported. And even when it's reported, it often goes unpunished. But here's a sorry fact. We're mesmerized by such crimes: they have become a form of mass culture entertainment, and a cover story for all kinds of fears. More children suffer from other forms of abuse: beatings, torture, starvation and neglect.[1] Why do these interest us less? Why do they interest journalists, novelists, scriptwriters, directors, producers and audiences less?

Perhaps they are harder to identify with, which makes them even scarier, more alien and maybe more revolting. Most of us can't imagine starving or beating a child into a stupor. We can't or don't want to imagine being treated that way by a parent. We all know something about the primal need to have caring and protective parents. Yet we remember what it was like to view adults as Olympians, powerful but unpredictable, beneficent and sometimes cruel. We know what it's like to feel helpless before adults, helpless because we love and hate them, want to yield and want to rebel. All of these memories and feelings become part of our sexuality. They are also part of what goes on when an adult sexually abuses a child. Statistically, the most frequent abusers of children are family members. Next come trusted adults: the family friend, teacher or mentor. Michael Jackson as alleged abuser falls into this category. His circumstances do the rest: the solitary voyage into oddness; the narcissism; the refusal to acknowledge that sleeping with children seems peculiar or perverse; even the insistence that only children deserve his love and trust, only children are innocent and honorable, only children want nothing from you.

Loving children is one thing. Elevating them beyond all adults—setting them up as a sacred species—is another. Children aren't wholly innocent or honorable. Children want many things from you. And adolescents of twelve, thirteen, and fourteen aren't children anymore, not altogether. They're betwixt and between. They're infantile and precociously adult. They have sexual desires, impulses they want to act on and test. I am not trying to turn Michael Jackson's accuser, Gavin Arvizo, into a youthful seducer. I am trying to say that there was almost no public acknowledgment of these everyday facts, known to anyone who has had a child, spent time with children or been a child. There was plenty of private talk, of course, and some blog talk. But blogs give us anonymity, and that

114

means we don't have to censor ourselves or risk being censored. (Trashed, yes, but not censored.)

When the notorious Martin Bashir documentary, *Living with Michael Jackson,* aired in 2003, a worldly acquaintance of mine told me that he had looked at Jackson and Gavin Arvizo sitting side by side, holding hands, and thought, "They're in love." I'm sure they were: all of Michael Jackson's relations with young people are romances. Children and adolescents are always falling in love with charismatic adults who speak to their secret self, some grief or private longing, some quirk of temper no one else gets. And these adults—parents, teachers, family friends—can abuse that power. For years, people disturbed by Michael Jackson's mutating looks and his suspicious and unself-conscious affinity for children would reassure themselves by saying, "But he loves children. Look at all the good things he does for children. Look at his charities and his generosity. He pays needy children's medical bills; he spends time with dying children whose dearest wish is to meet him; remember how he supported little Ryan White as he lay dying from AIDS?" Consider the songs and videos: "We Are the World," "Heal the World," "What More Can I Give?" Yet, in the wake of the 1993 sexual abuse charge, this new one took Michael Jackson even further beyond the pale. He was now an unconscionable, dangerous freak, a nefarious outsider, a despoiler of innocence deserving of punishment to the full extent of the law.

The short film for the song *Ghosts* was released in 1996, three years after the first charges of sexual molestation had been brought against Jackson by Thomas Sneddon, and two years after an out-of-court settlement ended the case. It is clearly a fable about the war—of words and of worlds—between these two men (based on a "concept" Jackson developed with the maestro of family horror, Stephen King). The Sneddon figure is the Mayor of Normal Valley, first seen leading a band of parents and children to the castle of the Maestro, who has been scaring the children with his tricks and tales. ("Neat stuff that's supposed to be a secret," as one boy says.)

Ghosts is stuffed with familiar, ever-compelling horror images. The parents carry torches to the castle, like the villagers in *Frankenstein*. The castle is a cavernous Poe-like dwelling with heavy brocade curtains and suits of armor. Lightning flashes; a raven flaps its wings; thunder cracks and doors slam shut, closing the intruders in. The Maestro appears, first as a skeleton in a black robe, then as Michael Jackson in a white shirt with a single row of ruffles, a white T-shirt, black pants and black shoulder-length hair.

The Mayor calls the Maestro a freak and orders him to leave town. The Maestro challenges the Mayor ("Are you scared now?"), twisting his face into masks that are part ghoul, part nineteenth-century black minstrel. "Did you think I was alone? Meet the family," he adds, and summons forth creatures who shape themselves into the skeletons of antique courtiers, ladies and jesters. The skeletons dance with African squats and robotic rotating knees and shoulders, with flamenco stamps and Native American stomps up the walls and across the balcony, cluster around a golden chandelier and drift lyrically down. Then (surely a reference to the gossip about his plastic surgeries), the Maestro tears his face off to reveal a skull. Later he bends down and, starting from his feet, tears off his whole body. Now he is Mister Bones in a Walpurgisnacht minstrel show.

This is a tormented film. The Maestro does violence to himself, then—through spirit possession—enters the Mayor's body, which pops and spins clumsily, as Michael sings of treachery and martyrdom, chants "Who gave you the right to scare my family?" and keens "Tell me, are you the ghost of jealousy?" His arm pops through the anguished Mayor's stomach and holds up a mirror. "Who's the freak now?" he taunts, and leaves the body in a rush of white flame.

"Do you still want me to go?" he asks, restored to his Maestro/Michael self. And when the Mayor says yes, he cracks his head on the floor and crumbles to brown, then black-and-white dust. But one more transformation gives the villain his cartoonish comeuppance, and the Maestro a happily ever after surrounded by joyful children and compliant parents.

When the credits roll, we discover that Michael Jackson played the Mayor, lumbering about, sneering threats in a flat, heavy voice and vanishing. Nine years later, the prosecutor of normal Santa Maria County will all but vanish after the trial, leaving Michael to whatever future he chooses in whatever sumptuous setting.

THOMAS MESEREAU, defense attorney: The high-profile, high-rent defense lawyer is a type as secure in our mythology as the cowboy. The hero of the type is a Clarence Darrow sort, defending people who are clearly innocent or who fight for clearly understood principles. (The villain? The villain is a legal mercenary who defends the morally suspect at both ends of the economic spectrum: the undeserving rich and the undeserving poor.) Novelists like John Grisham and Scott Turow still supply portraits of valiant defense lawyers snatching truth from the jaws of corporate and government chicanery. And there is a line of television series stretching from the valiant father-and-son team of the 1960s' *The Defenders* through the practical but still honorable team on the 1980s' *L.A. Law*. But *Law & Order* has turned prosecutors into our ethical, psychologically complex heroes. Since the 1990s, popular shows about defense lawyers, like *The Practice* or even the whimsical *Ally McBeal,* have offered characters with interesting psyches and questionable ethics.

How can it be otherwise given real-life defense lawyers like F. Lee Bailey, Melvin Belli, and Johnnie Cochran? High-profile, high-handed, fast-talking, eager to display their smarts in a way that brings back unpleasant memories of the college smart-ass. Here is Mark Geragos, let go by Jackson because he can't work on the case full-time: he's too busy defending Scott Peterson, the man charged with killing his wife and their unborn child. Here is Thomas Mesereau, free to give his all to Jackson because he no longer works for Robert Blake, charged with conspiring to murder and murdering his ex-wife. Mesereau is tall and stocky, with big broad shoulders and a starched curtain of white, almost shoulder-length hair. Unlike Sneddon, he thrives on press attention. When things are going well, he shows a touch of theatrical courtliness. When things aren't, he becomes crisp and insistent, as if to suggest: "Your assumptions are incorrect; your comment is overruled."

General opinion of Mesereau is high, meaning he is seen as smart, tenacious and ruthless when questioning witnesses. He also knows how to create the kind of courtroom drama we have come to expect: give pace and momentum to the exchanges; shift tone (from harsh, even bullying, to reflective and inquiring); change direction in midstream to catch witnesses off guard and reveal their lies and evasions under pressure. To put it more harshly, he knows how to bring out and show off the worst in people: the sullen smart aleck in Gavin Arvizo, the alleged victim; the slippery answers of the ex-Neverland employees who sued Jackson when they were fired and took their stories of his alleged sexual misdeeds to tabloids or lawyers instead of the police or social workers. He understands how to keep spectators on his side—or seduce them into feeling they should stay in his good graces. An aggressive line of questioning will suddenly give way to a wisecrack, a kind of aside to the audience that makes them feel superior. After Janet Arvizo, the mother of the alleged victim, claims that she never left Neverland to get a leg wax at a local spa during the time she was supposed to be imprisoned there, she refuses to look at the spa receipt and snaps, "I'm telling you, it was only a leg wax," then points at Jackson and adds, "I'm telling you, he has the ability to choreograph everything." "And how about you?" asks Mesereau. Later he gets her to admit she lied under oath when she brought a suit against JCPenney and won a $25,000 settlement from them. Then he asks about her appearance in the video Michael Jackson made to rebut Martin Bashir's infamous documentary. She had done "an inadequate job," she tells him, because "I'm a poor actress." "Oh, I think you're a good one," comes his reply.

Thomas Mesereau's postverdict press appearances

are models of well-crafted restraint. Commentators are prepared for triumphant showboating. Instead, Mesereau takes his cue from the quiet exit of the Jackson family. He looks relieved rather than gleeful. When he speaks to the press later, he assumes a posture of gratefulness. He talks about the work that went into the case and about what Jackson has gone through; he thanks his colleagues. Michael Jackson is a great gentleman, he says: kind, very well read, generous. He is proud to have worked with him. The television talking-head lawyer-commentators observe that, although he was a successful attorney before the case began, there is no telling how far he can go.

THE JURY: In late February of 2005, twelve jurors are selected from a pool of two hundred and fifty North County, California, residents. Their race is of the utmost importance to the public. Since only about 2 percent of North County is black—a stark contrast to Los Angeles, where the O.J. Simpson trial took place—it should be no surprise that the jury is made up of seven whites, four Latinos and one Asian. Alternate jurors rarely merit public attention, but this time it is duly noted, time and again, that one alternate is black. Polls show that most whites now feel reassured about the likelihood of a fair trial while most blacks are suspicious. And since eight of the jurors are women, gender also becomes a topic of intense speculation.

Reports and urban legends spread across the Internet. Haven't surveys shown that women jurors convict less often than men? That women are more likely to be sympathetic to celebrities? Or, on the other hand, that mothers might judge an accused child molester even more harshly than fathers?

Capsule profiles of the jury of Michael Jackson's "peers" are quickly offered in a chatty "these are our fellow citizens" style. Juror number 11 (Latino male, twenty) is "single with no children, and has a disabled mother. Says he is a *Simpsons* fan and doesn't really watch television news. Lists his job as an assistant head cashier." Juror number 7 (white male, twenty-one) is "a student with a high school degree who lives in Santa Maria. He is a wheelchair user. His father has served in the U.S. Air Force. A keen motor sports fan, he dreams of becoming a sports journalist." Juror number 4 (white female, fifty-two) is a "former computer programmer and systems analyst who also used to be a high school math teacher. She now says she is a homemaker with two teenage children, married to a university researcher." And so on: juror number 2 (Latino male, sixty-three) is a horseman with "a passion for Western art." Juror number 10 (white female, forty-five) is a supermarket worker with three children, ages fourteen to twenty-six.

Michael Jackson's peers? Who might they be?

JANET ARVIZO, mother of the alleged victim: Even
as Thomas Sneddon puts Michael Jackson on trial,
Thomas Mesereau puts the mother of his accuser on
trial. The official trial of Michael Jackson turns into the
unofficial trial of Janet Arvizo, along with the mothers
of every other child who had ever spent time in
Michael Jackson's bed. Why would they let their children spend days and weeks unsupervised at Neverland? Why would they let their children enter Michael
Jackson's bedroom, especially after the 1993 accusa-
tions and the out-of-court settlement? Why would
they compromise themselves by accepting his gifts and
credit card privileges?

Janet Arvizo's five days of testimony come in week
eleven of the trial. In the five weeks that follow, the
prosecution loses its momentum and its moral credi-
bility. Gavin Arvizo has charged Michael Jackson with
sexual abuse. Now it seems there is a history of abuse
in the Arvizo family. But abuse of whom by whom?
Janet Arvizo says she was beaten by her first husband,
the father of her three children. The daughter says she
was sexually abused by him. But, pressed in court, she
admits that she didn't remember this until she heard
her mother say it. The sons have accused their father
of physical abuse in a police report. But Gavin has
also accused his mother of abusing him: a welfare
worker investigated his claim and, pressed by Thomas

Mesereau, Mrs. Arvizo pleads the Fifth Amendment. The effect is to make all charges of abuse look fuzzy, more the result of hysteria, of emotional conflicts, than of fact.

Now for Janet Arvizo's appearance and manner. If Michael Jackson represents celebrity vulgarity, Janet Arvizo represents working-class tackiness. She comes to court in a pink suit for her first day of testimony, her face dramatically covered with a trench coat. Once inside, she treats the jurors as if she were in group therapy with them. "Please don't judge me," she begins. She describes how she has seen Michael Jackson lick her son's forehead like a cat. Here is one reporter's account of her testimony: " 'I had not slept in so long,' the witness said through tears. She mimicked the licking action on her arm—'Like this, over and over'—and said it occurred on a late-night flight from Miami to Los Angeles, when her 13-year-old son was asleep next to the King of Pop. 'I thought it was me. I thought I was seeing things. Everybody was asleep.' "[2]

She throws out courtroom protocol by interrupting Mesereau and challenging his questions. (Only lawyers are expected to intrude in that way.) Had her testimony been credible, this might have worked in her favor, struck a populist blow with the jury and the press. Instead it makes her look belligerent and shifty. After all, she has profited from her children's stay at Neverland. She is a *celebritista*. She insists on calling actors whom she had reached out to, George Lopez and Chris Tucker, "George" and "Chris." She says the white car Michael Jackson gave her "looked just like O.J. Simpson's." Her account of frantic calls to her mother while supposedly trapped at Neverland is less compelling than the shopping expeditions she has made during that period. "I tried to drop clues," she says about the calls to her mother. "I figured all this was going to be resolved by God's miracles. I sneaked in clues, so that one day this puzzle could be figured out."³ Michael Jackson has proven that he can be every bit as alienating when he speaks at length. But he is utterly silent in the courtroom.

Certain moments are crucial for the jurors. They speak of them in the press conference that follows the verdict. At one point, Janet Arvizo turned to the Latino jury foreman, snapped her fingers a few times, said, "You know how our culture is," and winked. "No," he tells the reporters, "that's not how our culture is." "I thought, 'Don't snap your fingers at me, lady,' " says the juror everyone calls the Grandmother. (Later the Grandmother will announce plans to market DON'T SNAP YOUR FINGERS AT ME, LADY T-shirts.) A third juror poses the ultimate parents' question and calls it her turning point: What kind of parents would let their children do what Janet Arvizo let hers do?

It is never satisfying to watch an entire culture shift blame—blame that has become mass entertainment—

from one person to another. It is never to be trusted. Clearly, Janet Arvizo was not the best of parents. Still, an empathetic prosecutor—one with a sense of social and emotional complexities—could have done better by her. A thoughtful prosecutor might have tried to make sense of her life, make her understandable if not quite sympathetic. How did this catch-as-catch-can life, the first marriage and divorce, affect her as she scrambled to beat the welfare system? Why had she tried to turn every piece of bad judgment or bad luck (Gavin's shoplifting at JCPenney or his being stricken with cancer) into a confidence game? What were the roots of her manic need for attention, her boasts and self-pity, her swings from pious anger to defiance? Of course, she should never have let her children loose at Neverland or treated it like her private fantasy island. This could have been used to make her son Gavin seem that much more of a victim: alone, in fragile health, looking for an adult to believe in when his own mother was like another bratty, needy child.

What kind of parent would let her child share a bed with any adult who is not a relative? Think for a minute how many adults in this country do share beds with children. Think how many siblings of different ages share beds. The Jackson brothers did when they were young and poor; so do lots of others. This isn't limited to poor people in small quarters; that's one of the reasons why sexual abuse crosses all social, ethnic, racial, religious and national borders. Stories abound of lonely parents—widows, divorced mothers and fathers—who shared beds with children past what one would consider the appropriate age. Often no molestation is involved (emotional claustrophobia, yes, but not molestation). Yet think of how often these people manage to abuse children, which goes unnoticed or unacknowledged by other family members who consider themselves to be far more loving and responsible than Janet Arvizo.[4]

DEBBIE ROWE, ex-wife of Michael Jackson, mother of two of his children: Debbie Rowe's testimony begins on April 25, ten days after Janet Arvizo's has ended. Call it the double maternal blow for the prosecution's hopes. They expect her to excoriate Jackson, but she praises him. It doesn't help that Sneddon and his team are unable to hide their shock and chagrin. Why would she want to help her ex-husband? asks prosecuting attorney Ron Zenon. "I promised him I would always be there for Michael and the children," answers Rowe. If you recall that she threatened to sue Michael for custody of those children a few months back, you are free to decide that a sentimental thread still binds the pair. After all, who but a wife and husband know exactly what has gone on in their relationship?

On her first day of testimony, Rowe states simply:

"We've been friends and we were married." No self-serving claims, no grandiosity. It can fit into a frame people understand, the frame of a marriage that went wrong—and probably should never have happened. There are so many marriages like that. "We never shared a home," Rowe tells the court, and beyond that she refuses to go. "My personal life was my personal life and no one's business," she declares. In a trial that leaves no other private detail undisclosed or undiscussed, what a relief this must be! How honorable it must look. And it begins to give Michael Jackson an aura of normalcy. He is an ex-husband and a parent. Like other ex-husbands and parents, his marriage hasn't worked out; he and his wife have gone through bad patches. But here she is, when he is accused of all sorts of sick, ugly acts, testifying on his behalf. She certainly does not seem like the kind of woman who would put her children in harm's way.

Many people have felt sorry for Debbie Rowe ever since she married Michael Jackson. They knew divorce was inevitable. Didn't *she*? She is the hefty, forthright girl next door—not the glamour girl, but the one you took for granted. She's likable and appears competent. Of course she made a good nurse for a plastic surgeon. Her unassuming manner, and her wholesome looks, must have been soothing to people in the midst of remaking themselves. It's easy to imagine her making patients like Michael follow the doctor's orders and feel good about themselves and their future. To some, their marriage proved he was gay: no straight man with power and prestige would marry her, it was assumed. To others it proved how desperately insecure he was. The racial inferiority complex: having first wed a hottie, daughter of the King of Rock and Roll, he now marries a white woman who will never leave him because he's the best she can hope to get! The social inferiority complex: he marries a woman who is dazzled by his wealth and power, having spent her adult life in a service profession where she got to see, but never mix with, the stars. The emotional inferiority complex: he marries a woman who will comfort and care for him, but is neither complicated enough to understand him nor entitled to demand his attention.

Rowe had appeared in Michael Jackson's rebuttal video disputing his portrayal in the Bashir documentary. Hadn't her supportive remarks been scripted? Assistant DA Ron Zenon asks. No, she answers in a brisk, forthright, "I'm the neighbor you can trust" way. His handlers—whom she later calls "opportunistic vultures"—had offered her a script, but she turned them down. "I didn't want anyone to be able to come back to me and say my interview was rehearsed. As Mr. Jackson knows, no one can tell me what to say." This last remark is the topper. Here's spunk, a little bit of true grit for you—not just your ordinary girl who's been used, then tossed aside by a superstar. She has somehow gone her own way. She has thrown down a few challenges of her own. Just what they were, no one can imagine, especially since she tells the court that she has not seen her children for years and still hopes to; that she considers Michael her friend and "wanted to get reacquainted" and hoped perhaps that the video would open the way. Nevertheless, in terms of the drama, Debbie Rowe plays as a person who still values her integrity. This is an image we all like to have of ourselves. This is why we may let it override a lot of circumstantial evidence.

THE MEDIA: The media is an overstocked mall of information and conjecture: 2,200 journalists cover the trial. Reporters peddle facts and rumors alike. The general tone? We're savvy observers who know how and when to be cynical. He's a sorry creature, a narcissist and possibly a madman (albeit shrewd at times: he still knows how to manipulate the court proceedings). Whatever the outcome, his career is probably over. We all suspect he's guilty, and if he's not guilty of every charge, he's guilty of behavior that makes him look guilty.

CNN's Nancy Grace is a former prosecutor with a hit talk show. Grace treats crime like small-town gossip. She is the last word on everybody's wrongdoings, an approach heightened by her southern twang, poufed hair and vehemently plucked eyebrows.

Grace declares Jackson guilty from the start and shapes all news to that opinion. She scolds and interrupts CNN reporters at the trial. She commiserates with the psychologist who explains why Michael Jackson is a pedophile. The night of the verdict, she interviews one of the jurors, questions his claims to rational judgment and ends by sneering, "How are you going to feel the next time you see him with his new *little friend*." She rarely fails to begin sentences with "I know when I was a prosecutor . . ." Unmentioned is the fact that when she was a prosecutor, the U.S. Court of Appeals for the Eleventh Circuit censured her on grounds that she knowingly withheld evidence that was favorable to a defendant.

Feature writers turn courtroom details into a portrait of absurdity. Mesereau's long white hair; Sneddon's huff-and-puff glower; the fans outside the courtroom who declare, "Michael was brought here on earth to do something special," or exchange fisticuffs over who loves him more. The standby metaphors are the circus and the freak show. The standard lecture goes: We Americans need to realize that our obsession with celebrities is unhealthy. If the trial does nothing else, hopefully it will teach us that. Occasionally a writer takes sharper aim and calls the trial a spectacular diversion that keeps reporters from covering the kinds of scandals and crises Americans need to be obsessed by—the war in Iraq, for instance. A week after the June 16, 2005, verdict, Stephen King points out for *Entertainment Weekly* that "more than 2000 newspeople covered the Jackson trial—which is only a few hundred more than the number of American servicemen and women who have died in Iraq." He adds: "And if you tell me that news doesn't belong in *Entertainment Weekly*, I respond by saying Michael Jackson under a black umbrella doesn't belong on the front page of the *New York Times*."

Few are as forthright. At regular intervals during the four-month trial, journalists declare that everyone expected the trial to be a media blockbuster, but it isn't. This must be a way for them to distance themselves from their assignment, for, all in all, the trial *is* a blockbuster. Its progress is covered, in minutest detail, by all major newspapers and TV news shows. There are reports on Jackson's finances and the tourist boom for Santa Barbara; the inevitable features on Jackson's career and family; reports on which celebrities support him (the Godfather of Soul himself, James Brown, emphatically declares the whole thing a setup; Usher is more cautious but respectful of Jackson's artistry and legal rights). There are stories meant to heighten the doom-laden atmosphere (one of Michael's emergency visits to the hospital had dislodged another patient, who later died). There are stories on the sad end of celebrities who were tarnished or destroyed by scandal (Fatty Arbuckle was ruined, Errol Flynn struggled, Jerry Lee Lewis and Chuck Berry rebounded somewhat).

Only the *Enquirer* and the *Star* offer guilt-free vulgarity set against a Hollywood backdrop. In one issue of *The National Enquirer* his picture is just one of four that frames a lead story headlined "Jessica Simpson Link to Rape Scandal." "Jacko on Drugs During Trial!" shares space with "Demi Pregnancy Nightmare," "Tom Hanks Cancer Ordeal" and "Sharon Stone Sends Boyfriend Packing for Sexy Beach Boy!" Both papers run so many pictures of stars in the throes of plastic surgery that Michael's face becomes just another face in the crowd. Each week *The National Enquirer* reserves its back page for tales of ordinary people who've been surgically born again. The week its front-page headline reads "Jacko: Why He'll Walk Free" (an unsensational story about Thomas Mesereau's defense strategy); the back page headline reads: "Mom Was So Homely, People Thought She Was a Man!" So Mom's "caring daughters" contacted the producers of *Extreme Makeover* and now Mom looks like thousands of blond bachelorettes.

Almost every television show hires a lawyer to provide what is called expert trial analysis and commentary. Much of the "commentary" is intellectualized gossip. Court TV chooses a prosecutorial approach and wins big ratings. Viewers like debating whether reporter Diane Diamond is a spiteful harpy or a righteous avenger. True to its show-business roots, E! Entertainment Television decides to stage reenactments of key trial scenes. These are framed by roundtable discussions among four lawyers who trade impressions, debate strategies and tell us what to look for in each scene. The point is to blend the look of fact and the feel of fiction. Plus—because cameras have been banned from the courtroom—a touch of the forbidden.

THE SUMMATION: Why does Michael Jackson sleep with children, even if he doesn't sexually molest them? People who love Michael Jackson will talk about his terrible childhood: the beatings, the rumors of sexual abuse, the ceaseless rehearsing and performing from age five. And people convinced of his guilt or, at the very least, his insufferable narcissism will snap back: Lots of people had terrible childhoods; he should get over it. But he can't get over it. And he's not alone. The children Michael Jackson has made friends with share some crucial part of his background: poverty, isolation, some kind of ambition, emotional deprivation and, from Macaulay Culkin's father to Gavin Arvizo's mother, at least one exploitative parent. The world is full of people who cannot get over childhood damage or adult trauma. If they could, psychoanalysis, therapy and social work would not exist. Neither would all the forms of self-abuse and self-destruction ordinary people practice. At this point Michael Jackson's damage is equal to what his talent was, and that means it is extraordinary indeed. This is deeply upsetting to witness. Who wants to try and map that kind of compulsion and regression? Who wants to watch mental illness in panoramic close-up? What language is available to us when talking about it?

Within just three paragraphs of her book *An Unquiet Mind: A Memoir of Moods and Madness,* the psychiatrist and manic-depressive Kay Redfield Jamison uses three different terms: "mental illness," "madness" and "abnormal mental states and behavior."[5] She knows that unstable states of being unnerve people and create unstable language. "Mental illness" may sound patronizing, but at least it's clinical; "madness" in the wrong mouth amounts to a stigma. So, how do people talk about conditions, states of being, that wrench, confuse, disgust and scare them? People take refuge in the vernacular: it offers a form of mastery. Inventive. Brutally frank or slyly euphemistic. During the Jackson trial, the pallid, officious "mentally disturbed" showed up when a certain gravitas was required. But the vernacular was the irate pundit's favorite. Jackson was crazy, nuts, cracked or around the bend. He needed to get a grip. And of course he was "off the wall," wasn't he? The title of Jackson's first hit album as a solo performer was thrown back at him with near-triumphant sarcasm.

There was no narrative space for real talk about mental illness: what it looked like or felt like; its symptoms and causes; its many shades and consequences. The trial revealed an almost primitive refusal to examine any of this. The defense wanted to call a psychiatrist who would explain to the court why Jackson's book collection showed he did not fit the profile of a pedophile. But the prosecution threatened to call a psychiatrist who would study the same books and explain why he did. Both sides retreated. Articles would sometimes quote psychiatrists about his mental state during the trial—and the probability of his guilt or innocence—much as dermatologists had been asked their opinions as to whether or not he had vitiligo, and plastic surgeons queried as to how many operations his nose had endured. There was no reasonable discussion of how Jackson might be innocent of molestation, though not of gross emotional improprieties; how he might not be able to stop himself or take in how he was viewed by the rest of the world. Mental illness distorts and maims, but it does not have to be criminal.

It is a given of Michael Jackson's life that he cannot really connect to anyone but children. In his videos, children hold candles and sing with him about a world free of hatred; they flee war beneath his protective shadow. Children embody the innocence he was denied. And he is the all-powerful parent whom no human child can really have. Children give unconditional love. They are dependent, they must be cared for, and that gives the parental figure power along with responsibility. Is it possible that Michael Jackson sexually engages children? Yes. He compulsively reimagines the violation of his own innocence, then purifies himself with kind, caring acts. Isn't it just as possible that he is asexual? That he basks in that innocence and shelters it just as compulsively—that he is tempted but resists time and again? He sets the scene of his own violation, repeats the scenario but rewrites the ending. He rescues himself and the child. And yet, he experiences the excitement—the eros—of being tempted.[6]

"Please don't judge me / Just try to love me," Michael sings in the video *Have You Seen My Childhood?* He sits on a grassy knoll, arms wrapped around his knees. His hair is short and curly, like Peter Pan's. His face is rapt and full of wonder as he watches children—multiracial boys and girls—float through a starry sky in little boats. *If you want to know about my life, look at this video,* he has said. What does he see? What do we? A man who wants to be androgynous and beyond race? An artist of genius who has given us acute excitement and pleasure? A willful celebrity who wants everything his way, yet insists that everyone love him unconditionally? A man driven to shed his identity, while denying what pains him? Our man in the mirror? Or a creature we no longer wish to acknowledge?

Michael Jackson speaks to and for the monstrous child in us all.

Notes

Freaks

1. Adrienne Kennedy's 1962 play *Funnyhouse of a Negro* explores such multiple identities wonderfully.

2. J.M. Barrie, *Peter Pan in Kensington Gardens* (Oxford: Oxford University Press, 1999). This Oxford World Classics volume also contains *Peter and Wendy*, and has a fine introduction and detailed notes by Peter Hollindale.

3. Rachel Adams, *Sideshow, U.S.A.* (Chicago: University of Chicago Press, 2001). For analyses of Barnum, the freak show, the mythology of freaks, and the entertainment industry's use of racial, sexual, gender and age tropes, I am especially indebted to: Rachel Adams; Robert Bogdan, *Freak Show: Presenting Human Oddities for Amusement and Profit* (Chicago: University of Chicago Press, 1988); Joshua Gamson, *Freaks Talk Back: Tabloid Talk Shows and Sexual Nonconformity* (Chicago: University of Chicago Press, 1998); Constance Rourke, *Trumpets of Jubilee* (New York: Harcourt Brace, 1963); Rosemarie Garland Thomson, ed., *Freakery: Cultural Spectacles of the Extraordinary Body* (New York: New York University Press, 1996). This volume includes excellent essays by David Yuan on Michael Jackson, and by Lori Merish on Tom Thumb and Shirley Temple.

4. Sigmund Freud, "The Uncanny," in *The Uncanny: Experi-*

ments in Cyborg Culture. Ed. Bruce Grenville. (Vancouver: Vancouver Art Gallery, 2002).

5. After nineteen years with Barnum, Chang and Eng showed how well they could adapt to the environment of privileged white America. They retired to a plantation in North Carolina, where they raised crops, married sisters from good white families and produced twenty children between them.

6. Elizabeth Grosz, "Intolerable Ambiguity: Freaks at/as the Limit," in *Freakery: Cultural Spectacles of the Extraordinary Body.*

7. J.M. Barrie, *Peter and Wendy.*

8. Michael Jackson, *Moonwalk* (New York: Doubleday, 1998). Unless otherwise indicated, all Michael Jackson quotes are from *Moonwalk.* To Marjorie Garber, this anecdote "has something about it of the primal scene of show business." Garber, *Vested Interests* (New York: Routledge, 1997). Garber writes about Jackson and J.M. Barrie here and in *Vice Versa: Bisexuality and the Eroticism of Everyday Life* (New York: Simon & Schuster, 1995).

Home

1. There are many books about the Jackson family and about Michael Jackson: biographies, photo documentaries, purported exposés and hagiographies. There are Web sites as well. For trustworthy reporting, two of the most helpful books remain: Nelson George, *The Michael Jackson Story* (New York: Dell, 1984) and J. Randy Taraborrelli, *Michael Jackson: The Magic and the Madness* (New York: Ballantine Books, 1991). For photographs and year-by-year accounts of Jackson's recordings, films and videos, tours and appearances, there are: Adrian Grant, *Michael*

Notes

Jackson: Visual Documentary (New York: Omnibus Press, 2001); Darren Brooks and Billy Dancer, *Michael Jackson: An Exceptional Journey* (New Malden, UK: Chrome Dreams, 2002); Chris Cadman and Craig Halstead, *Michael Jackson: The Early Years* (Hertford, UK: Authors Online Ltd, 2002).

2. Most quotations from Jehovah's Witness literature and most of the historical background are from Barbara Grizzuti Harrison, *Visions of Glory: A History and a Memory of Jehovah's Witnesses* (New York: Simon & Schuster, 1978). The Witnesses also have an official Web site, watchtower.org. There are also sites that distribute information critical of the Witnesses and The Watchtower Society: watchtowerinformationservices.org includes academic papers and personal testimonies on such subjects as Witness finances and their policies on race and sexual abuse.

Star Child

1. Much fine work has been done on the history of blackface minstrelsy and black vaudeville, as well as on the aesthetics of black music, dance and culture. I found especially helpful: Annemarie Bean, ed., *Inside the Minstrel Mask: Readings in Nineteenth-Century Blackface Minstrelsy* (Middletown, Conn.: Wesleyan University Press, 1996); Tom Fletcher, *100 Years of the Negro in Show Business* (New York: Da Capo Press, 1984); Brenda Dixon Gottschild, *The Black Dancing Body* (New York: Palgrave Macmillan, 2003); Marc Anthony Neal, *Soul Babies: Black Popular Culture and the Post-Soul Aesthetic* (New York: Routledge, 2002); Marshall and Jean Stearns, *Jazz Dance: The Story of American*

Vernacular Dance (New York: Da Capo Press, 1994); Michele Wallace and Gina Dent, *Black Popular Culture* (Seattle, Wash.: Bay Press, 1992).

2. Tom Dardis, *Keaton* (New York: Limelight Editions, 1979).

3. Diana Serra Cary, *Jackie Coogan: The World's Boy King* (Lanham, Md.: Scarecrow Press, 2003).

4. Sammy Davis Jr. and Jane and Burt Boyar, *Yes I Can* (New York: Noonday Press, 1990).

5. Motown has been exhaustively chronicled from various points of view. My sources include: Peter Benjaminson, *The Story of Motown* (New York: Grove Press, 1979); Berry Gordy Jr., *To Be Loved: The Music, the Magic, the Memories of Motown* (New York: Warner Books, 1995); Nelson George, *Where Did Our Love Go: The Rise and Fall of the Motown Sound* (New York: Omnibus Press, 2003); Raynoma Gordy Singleton, *Berry, Me, and Motown* (New York: Contemporary Books, 1990).

Alone of All His Race, Alone of All Her Sex

1. Keith Haring, *Keith Haring: Journals* (London: Fourth Estate, 1996).

2. Tawil, Ezra. *The Making of Racial Sentiment: Slavery and the Birth of the Frontier Romance* (Cambridge and New York: Cambridge University Press, 2006).

3. Susan Fillin-Yeh, "Introduction," *Dandies: Fashion and Finesse in Art and Culture*, Susan Fillin-Yeh, ed. (New York: New York University Press, 2001).

4. I have been helped by the work of a number of writers and critics on gender, race and cultural representations, particularly: Virginia L. Blum, *Flesh Wounds: The Culture of Cosmetic*

Notes

Surgery (Berkeley: University of California Press, 2003); Susan Bordo, *Twilight Zones: The Hidden Life of Cultural Images from Plato to O.J.* (Berkeley: University of California Press, 1997); Thelma Golden, *Black Male: Representations of Masculinity in Contemporary American Art* (New York: Whitney Museum of American Art, 1994); Elizabeth Haiken, *Venus Envy: A History of Cosmetic Surgery* (Baltimore, Md.: The Johns Hopkins University Press, 1997); Victoria Pitts, *In the Flesh: The Cultural Politics of Body Modification* (New York: Palgrave Macmillan, 2003); Greg Tate, ed., *Everything but the Burden: What White People Are Taking from Black Culture* (New York: Broadway Books, 2003).

5. The entire passage reads: "The Negro has always been interested rather in expression than in action; interested in life itself rather than in its reconstruction or reformation. The Negro is, by natural disposition, neither an intellectual nor an idealist, like the Jew; nor a brooding introspective, like the East Indian; nor a pioneer and frontiersman, like the Anglo-Saxon. He is primarily an artist, loving life for its own sake. His *métier* is expression rather than action. He is, so to speak, the lady among the races" (John F. Callahan, ed., *The Collected Essays of Ralph Ellison* [New York: Modern Library, 2003]).

The Trial

1. National Clearinghouse on Child Abuse and Neglect Information, a service of The Children's Bureau Administration for Children and Families, U.S. Department of Health and Human Services.

2. Lisa Sweetingham, Court TV Web site (www.courttv. com), April 13, 2005.

3. Ibid., April 14, 2005.

4. The Los Angeles County prosecutor charged Janet Arvizo with five counts of welfare fraud and perjury on August 23, 2005, two months and ten days after Jackson's acquittal. She pleaded not guilty.

5. Jamison's books include: *Touched with Fire: Manic-Depressive Illness and the Artistic Temperament* (New York: Free Press, 1993). Another interesting book, for which Jamison wrote the foreword, is the journalist John Head's memoir and cultural survey, *Standing in the Shadows: Understanding and Overcoming Depression in Black Men* (New York: Broadway Books, 2004).

6. Two books that thoroughly examine the psychological consequences of abuse are: Judith Herman, *Trauma and Recovery* (New York: Basic Books, 1992) and Jody Messler Davies and Mary Gail Frawley, *Treating the Adult Survivor of Childhood Sexual Abuse: A Psychoanalytic Perspective* (New York: Basic Books, 1994).

Acknowledgments

A writer needs readers long before a book is published. Mine were exceptional and I thank them for their help at various stages: Ann Douglas, Nancy Gist, Elizabeth Kendall, Christine Carter Lynch and Gail Papp. It's impossible to write about a figure like Michael Jackson alone—he belongs to too many people. I am grateful for the insights and reactions of K.C. Arceneaux, Pio Cabada, Charlotte Carter, the Chicago Northeast-erners, Celia Epiotes, Helen Epstein, Judson Esty-Kendall, Ulrika Hallberg, Francesca Harper, Anthony Heilbut, Patrick Horrigan, Denise Jefferson, Alexandra Kendall, Adrienne Kennedy, Harry King, Joan Krevlin, Danzy Senna, Betty Shamieh and Laurie Woodard. Michael Mallick contributed his sensibility and wit along with his research. Claire Tamarkin Snyder was a delight to work with.

In September 2004, The African American Studies Department and The Larry Kramer Initiative for Lesbian and Gay Studies at Yale cosponsored a conference called "Regarding Michael Jackson: Performing Racial,

Gender and Sexual Differences: Center Stage." It was fortuitous; I was helped and encouraged by the readings of Jackson I heard there. I am also grateful to Erin Chapman and Yale's 2004–2005 African American Studies Seminar Series on Black Feminism for inviting me to read a chapter in progress.

Finally, I thank my editor, Erroll McDonald. His mind and his eye are extraordinary. He is an artist at what he does.